YALE LANGUAGE SERIES

Talking

A Brazilian Portuguese Pronunciation Workbook

Yale University Press

Mário A. Perini

Pontifícia Universidade Católica, Minas Gerais

Brazilian

New Haven & London

Publisher: Mary Jane Peluso
Production Controller: Laura Burrone
Editorial Assistant: Gretchen Rings
Designer: Nancy Ovedovitz
Marketing Manager: Timothy J. Shea
Illustrations: Juliane Assis
Audio Engineering: Felipe Amorim
Music: Marcus Vinicius de Freitas

Set in Adobe Garamond type with Meta display by The Composing Room of Michigan, Inc. Printed in the United States of America by Sheridan Books.

Library of Congress Cataloging-in-Publication Data

Perini, Mário A.
Talking Brazilian : a Brazilian Portuguese pronunciation workbook / Mário A. Perini
p. cm. — (Yale language series)
ISBN 0-300-10021-3 (alk. paper)
1. Portuguese language—Brazil—Pronunciation. 2. Portuguese language—Textbooks for foreign speakers—English.
I. Title. II. Series.
PC5444.P48 2003
469.7′98—dc21   2003049683

A catalogue record for this book is available from the British Library.

The paper in this book meets the guidelines for permanence and durability of the Committee on Production Guidelines for Book Longevity of the Council on Library Resources.

10 9 8 7 6 5 4 3 2 1

To Peggy Sharpe,
a true friend
and living proof that English speakers can acquire perfect Brazilian
pronunciation

Contents

Acknowledgments   ix

Introduction   xi

Lesson 1: [i, ə]; [b, f, g, s, ʃ, v, z, ʒ, m, n]   1

Lesson 2: [-ˈiːjə]   4

Lesson 3: [tʃ, dʒ]   6

Lesson 4: [u, w]   9

Lesson 5: [ɛ]   12

Lesson 6: [a]   15

Lesson 7: [j]   18

Lesson 8: [p, t, k]   20

Lesson 9: [ɔ]   23

Lesson 10: [d, l, h]   26

Lesson 11: [w] (again)   29

Lesson 12: [e, ej]   32

Lesson 13: [o, ow]   37

Lesson 14: [ɾ]   42

Lesson 15: [ʌ]   45

Lesson 16: [ʌ̃]   49

Lesson 17: [ẽ, õ]   53

Lesson 18: [ĩ, ũ]   57

Lesson 19: [ɉ̃]   62

Lesson 20: [ʎ̃ w̃]   67

Lesson 21: Triphthongs and vocalic sequences   72

Lesson 22: Inserted [i]   76

Lesson 23: Proparoxytones   80

Lesson 24: Oxytones   84

Lesson 25: Joining words: final **m, l,** and **r**   88

Lesson 26: Joining words: vowel reduction   92

Lesson 27: Stress patterns in cognates   95

Lesson 28: Intonation: declarative sentences vs.

      yes-no questions   100

Lesson 29: Intonation: declarative sentences vs.

      topicalized sentences   104

Lesson 30: Intonation: wh-questions   107

Lesson 31: Intonation: choice questions,

      echo-questions, and tag-questions   111

Lesson 32: Dialogues to memorize   117

Key to the Exercises   123

Translations of the Dialogues   125

Acknowledgments

I would like to thank several people who provided criticism, guidance, and other help during the preparation of this workbook.

First of all, I thank my wife, Lúcia, who read the whole text and gave precious advice from her many years of experience as a foreign-language teacher.

I am grateful to Peggy Sharpe, chair of the Modern Languages Department at the University of Mississippi at Oxford, who made it possible for me to work there during the 2001–2002 and 2002–2003 school years, teaching Portuguese to American students. I would like to thank and acknowledge Jordano Quaglia, Yale University, who reviewed the manuscript.

My students both at the University of Illinois and at the University of Mississippi were the source of many insights about the real problems for English speakers learning Brazilian pronunciation.

Juliane Assis provided the excellent illustrations that enliven the book.

I also want to thank the staff put together to produce the CD: the Brazilian voices (Juliana Fulgêncio, Ivana Marzano, Fernando Perini, and Henrique Perini); the American voice (Suzanne Beaudette Drummond); the musician (Marcus Vinicius de Freitas); and the recording technician (Felipe Amorim). Stela Arnold helped with the English text.

Finally, I thank the staff of Yale University Press for their indispensable support and kindness.

Introduction

To the Teacher

Whoever teaches foreign languages knows that there are no magical formulas. Written exercises, oral practice, audiovisual and audio-oral resources, structural drills, communicative approaches—all these are useful, but none provides "the solution." In general, teachers make use of each method as they feel it to be appropriate. No substitute has been devised for the resourceful teacher seconded by the intelligent, hard-working student.

Is there a methodology that harmonizes perfectly with the current linguistic theories? My position, amply borne out by classroom experience, can be expressed in Anna Ciliberti's words: "The best methodology, the one that yields the most satisfactory results, is always a mixed methodology, difficult to define because its success dwells in the details, in the dosage, in flexibility . . .—features that are difficult to generalize" (*Manuale di Glottodidattica* [Florence: La Nuova Italia Editrice, 1994], 83; my translation). This does not mean that theory is irrelevant, just that its use in our activities must always be subordinated to the goals of language teaching. Ultimately every procedure will stand or fall according to the excellence of its results.

Since language teaching is essentially such a complex activity, teachers will do well to have at hand a variety of tools and to learn to employ them all. This book provides one such tool, aimed at perfecting students' pronunciation of Portuguese by means of exercises and drills.

Principles Underlying the Approach

A pronunciation workbook Some authors question the utility of a pronunciation workbook, often because they misunderstand the claims of Communicative Language Teaching and related methodologies, which are in fact perfectly compatible with a focus on phonological and phonetic accuracy. As an auxiliary resource, a pronunciation workbook is a very useful tool in language teaching, particularly at the early stages. Pronunciation skills are basically automatic; that is, pronunciation is one of those things that you do not really *know* until you forget about them. The acquisition of correct pronunciation—especially by adults—requires a great deal of practice, and that is what the exercises in this book provide.

The contrastive approach The approach adopted here may be defined as contrastive—another of the formulas once thought to provide a basis for "the solution" and later, just as wrongly, rejected by some as useless. Contrary to what some authors apparently believe, contrastive analysis is not connected in any essential way to behaviorist theories in linguistics or in psychology. It is neutral as to theoretical approach and assumes simply that a main source of the difficulties an adult encounters when learning a new language is interference between the features of that language and comparable features of his or her native language. For instance, we can predict that an English speaker will have some trouble with the gender of nouns in Portuguese (e.g., *mesa* 'table' is feminine, whereas *banco* 'bench' is masculine); with the pronunciation of nasal vowels; and with the structure of the (colloquial) relative clause *o casaco que eu viajei com ele* 'the coat I traveled with.' Such potential points of difficulty are identified by means of a contrastive analysis of the two languages.

For all its relevance, contrastive analysis does not solve all problems. Not *all* points in which the two languages differ will automatically become learning problems, nor are contrastive differences the only source of problems. The task of learning pronunciation is complex, and we should never put our trust blindly on any one resource. There is nothing simple about language learning and teaching.

The contrastive analysis of the native language with the language being learned is, however, *one* of the resources that authors and teachers must use when trying to devise more efficient language courses. And exercises and drills are indispensable in enabling adult students (as opposed to children up to about twelve) to develop fluent speech habits in a foreign language.

Differences among languages Some authors hold that foreign-language learners tend to concentrate on the aspects of the language that are essential for communication while neglecting the aspects that are of low utility. Apart from the vexed question of ascertaining with any reliability the utility of each element of a language, I think such an opinion is disproved in most cases. Rather, classroom experience shows that students are very often bogged down by those features of the foreign language that, regardless of their communicative utility, differ most markedly from related features in the students' native language. If it were otherwise, there would be no explanation for the trouble that native Portuguese speakers have in learning to aspirate initial voiceless consonants or to pronounce correctly the **r**'s in sequences like *Sorority Row*, nor their ease in pronouncing the **z** in *zebra*—which is difficult for speakers of Spanish, a language that lacks the **z** sound. Such contrastive differences loom particularly large in the area of pronunciation.

Fossilization A serious and often neglected aspect of language learning is that perfect pronunciation is *not* essential to communication; it is possible to speak and be understood in a foreign language even if one's pronunciation only approximates a native speaker's. As soon as basic communication is achieved, poor pronunciation habits may "fossilize": "The learner stops at a certain level of competence, sufficient for the needs of communication, and does not progress any more." Ciliberti explains further that fossilization "seems to be caused by the fact that the [learner] does not manage to analyze the incoming data, compare them with his own production, evaluate the differences, and finally formulate new hypotheses" (*Manuale,* 46, 174).

Fossilization helps account for the inability of many adults to acquire a good pronunciation of a foreign language. Doing serious work on pronunciation at the early stages of learning is important, therefore. If fossilization is inevitable, teachers must at least work with the students, and students must strive, to achieve pronunciation as close to native as possible.

Overall Organization

OVERVIEW

The sounds The present workbook consists mainly of exercises. Complete descriptions and explanations of all sounds in Portuguese and their orthographic representations are found in chapters 2–6 of my *Modern Portuguese: A Reference Grammar* (New Haven: Yale University Press, 2002). Although *Modern Portuguese* may be consulted as a reference, this workbook can be used independently. All crucial information is provided in the workbook or in the recording.

A systematic approach In this workbook the study of Brazilian Portuguese pronunciation is approached in a way that may be described as *progressive* and *contrastive*. Instead of beginning with complete sentences, that is, with all the phonetic and phonological complexity of normal utterances, I have classified every sound of the language, taking into account their clusterings and distribution in words and sentences, and introduced them according to the degree of difficulty they present to the English-speaking student.

The intersection of English and Portuguese Students will begin practicing pronunciation with words composed of sounds that are virtually identical in English and Portuguese. In the first words, the sounds are placed in phonological environments as similar as possible to the ones in which they occur in English. New environments are gradually introduced. Eventually the student is learning Portuguese sounds that have no correlates in English.

Vowel and semivowel pronunciation For unknown reasons, some sound sequences that are present in both English and Portuguese cause pronunciation problems for many English speakers. Let me mention in particular certain vowel and semivowel sequences like the ones found in *maioria* 'majority' and *continuar* 'to continue.' I include exercises to practice these.

DESIGN OF THE LESSONS

Each sound is the subject of special drills that emphasize listening and speaking in turn. The systematic approach enables students to build adequate pronunciation without overloading their attention with too many unknown sounds at once. The accompanying CD provides models of native speech to be imitated. It includes all Portuguese words and sentences given in the text. The thirty-two lessons provide a complete course in the pronunciation of Brazilian Portuguese.

- *Lessons 1–3* focus on words made up of vowels and consonants identical in English and Portuguese. The exercises present them in phonological environments that match their distribution in English.
- *Lesson 4* introduces the vowel [u], which is similar, but not identical to, English **u** in *rule* and thus requires special attention.
- *Lesson 5* presents the vowel [ɛ], which is identical to English **e** in *less* but appears in different environments. In Portuguese it may, for instance, appear at the end of a word. After completing this lesson, students will have been introduced to all

sounds of the language, as well as all sound sequences that may be difficult to produce.

- *Lessons 6–32* deal with intonation, stress, rhythm, and sound changes in context—the rest of the elements that, once learned, make speakers sound like native Brazilians.

In certain cases Portuguese utilizes phonological oppositions that are absent in English, and these are treated in special drills. An example is the opposition between oral versus nasal vowels, for which I provide exercises based on the perception and production of minimal pairs (*mudo* [u] / *mundo* [ũ], *pau* [aw] / *pão* [ãw], *vi* [i] / *vim* [ĩ], etc.).

LEARNING THE SOUNDS

At the head of each lesson is a list of the sounds or special contexts being introduced. The sounds are given in phonetic transcription and then briefly described. I compare them with English sounds where applicable. The descriptions, in boxes marked with a pushpin, are sometimes taken more or less verbatim from *Modern Portuguese.*

The explanations are to be taken only as memory aids. Students should work primarily by imitating the models provided on the CDs and by the teacher. No description or explanation can replace aural perception and memorization. Still, explanations can be useful given the difficulties students may experience in perceiving phonetic differences between the languages (the "blind spots" of aural perception)—as when an English-speaking student fails to perceive the difference between Portuguese oral and nasal vowels and thus cannot tell *vi* '(I) saw' from *vim* '(I) came,' or when the student pronounces the Portuguese *dei* (with a dental consonant) as identical to the English *day* (with an alveolar consonant). Here the role of the teacher is crucial, for students are often unable to overcome such deficiencies by themselves.

After the sound list, I give some words or short phrases to be pronounced in isolation following the recorded models. With each word or phrase is a phonetic transcription plus a gloss (sometimes very approximate). Where appropriate, I provide minimal pairs to help students perceive sound differences that do not occur in English.

Only one phonetic transcription is given for each form, but in some cases other pronunciations are also possible and equally acceptable. For instance, *reis* 'kings' and *rês* 'head of cattle' are assigned different pronunciations (['heːjs] and ['heːs], respectively); but for many speakers they are homophonous, both being pronounced ['heːjs]. These alternatives are not given in the material included here; some of them are described in chapters 2–4 of *Modern Portuguese*.

Every lesson includes a set of sentences and phrases that provide models of intonation patterns and the way words are joined in normal speech, allowing students to practice fluency with longer stretches of discourse. The repetition of ready-made sentences, carefully planned to include only sounds already studied, has the advantage of freeing students' attention to concentrate on the pronunciation, including intonation, following the recorded models.

In the first three lessons, I include some additional phrases and sentences for advanced students who already have some proficiency but still need to work on their pronunciation. Beginners should skip over all the exercises marked "For Advanced Students."

LEARNING THE DIALOGUES

To take the practice in normal speech one step further, I also provide, starting with Lesson 15, some short dialogues, to be memorized and performed as little plays by pairs of students. At that stage the student will probably be able to understand these dialogues (perhaps with the help of the teacher). A student should never learn by rote a text he or she does not fully understand. Learning a series of sounds by themselves leads nowhere.

Memorizing texts may be viewed by some as an old-fashioned activity, but in my opinion, it is very useful in acquiring good pronunciation of a foreign language. Memorization frees the mind from the burden of building the utterance and makes it easier for the student to focus on details of pronunciation—in particular, intonation, rhythm, and the fluent, natural linking of words in sentences.

All texts are recorded, providing a model to be followed. The first texts are planned to avoid some of the more difficult sounds and sound combinations, such as nasal vowels and diphthongs, triphthongs, and proparaoxytones, as well as very long words. These difficulties are gradually included in later texts, following their introduction in the lessons.

The texts are written in a rather colloquial register, to sound natural when spoken. In this I follow the general practice of modern Brazilian playwrights.

Some of the sentences in the lessons are used only in the spoken language (see chapter 1 of *Modern Portuguese* for the difference between spoken and written usage in Brazil). And if some of the sentences sound slightly funny, please remember that they were composed under severe phonological limitations: each sentence contains only sounds studied in previous lessons. The same applies to the selection of isolated words, so in a few cases I had to depart from the criterion of selecting high-frequency items in order to attend to the needs of phonological illustration.

SLURRING

In the recording the exercises are limited largely to the pronunciation of isolated words and short phrases. But an isolated word is one thing, and a word in its discursive context is quite another, phonetically speaking. Brazilians, like English speakers, are much given to slurring words, especially where the speaker feels that the context is sufficiently informative. Since practice in slurring in a workbook like this one would complicate it unduly, I have compromised in favor of relatively careful pronunciation, the pronunciation accepted as correct by all speakers and normal in slower styles of speech. This workbook is aimed at developing basic pronunciation skills.

Yet it must be said that slurring—a characteristic feature of fast speech—is an important phenomenon. Here a few examples.

- A word like *canto* ['kɐ̃ːtu], will be shortened to ['kɐ̃ː] when used before the preposition *de* in a noun phrase, as in *canto de passarinho* 'bird song,' where it is pronounced ['kɐ̃ːdʒipasaˈrĩːʲu], as if the phrase were *can'dipassarinho*.
- A long word like *eletrônico* may lose its two final (unstressed) syllables, which will at most be just whispered and nearly inaudible, because the word is long enough that the first part of the word is sufficient for identification.
- A word that was already employed in the discourse may occur in reduced form when repeated, because it is easily identified from context.

All these reductions are subject to rules, which may relate to syntax or pragmatics as well as phonology. Their inclusion in a workbook will have to wait until the subject is researched as it deserves.

In the listening-comprehension exercises students must bear in mind that a word is identified not merely by its phonetic and phonological shape but also by the predictions the hearers make as they listen. If I say in English *I'll have a lettuce and tomato salad,* the word *salad* may sound like *solid,* yet no confusion will result, because hearers process the utterance at all levels simultaneously and know that *solid* would make no sense. The reading *solid* does not even arise in a hearer's mind. This mechanism of processing utterances at several levels is essential; trying to identify every word on the basis of its phonetic shape alone would block comprehension. Therefore, even though this workbook provides a basis for developing listening comprehension, for all-round improvement students must work at other aspects of comprehension by other means—among other things, by the acquisition of a large vocabulary.

ADDITIONAL CONSIDERATIONS

Variations in pronunciation Brazilian pronunciation is quite uniform across the country, but there are regional differences, which, though comparatively small, must be taken into account in teaching and learning Brazilian Portuguese. The basis for the exercises in this book is the pronunciation of schooled people in the Southeastern part of the country, which may be considered a compromise between the more extreme varieties of the Northeast and the South. It is also the pronunciation most commonly used in television and radio broadcasts. Since even in the Southeast pronunciation is not totally uniform, some decisions had to be made as to which variants to include in the exercises. Instead of registering all regional or social variants, which might lead students into confusion and uncertainty, I have systematically selected one form for each word. For instance, the pronunciation I give for syllable-final **s** is [s], instead of [ʃ], because the former is less limited regionally. Fortunately, the variation of pronunciation in Brazil is generally slight enough not to seriously impair comprehension even for beginning students.

Phonetic transcriptions The transcriptions given are broad phonetic; that is, without going into detail, they often represent even sound differences that are not linguistically significant (as with the difference in pronunciation of **t** as [tʃ] before [i], and as [t] elsewhere). Minor differences are best learned from live speakers or from recordings. Stressed vowels are all long, but I indicate their length, mainly as a reminder, because English-speaking students have a tendency to pronounce some of them short. (Lengths do vary slightly; final stressed vowels are usually shorter than nonfinal ones, for example. But such fine distinctions need not be represented in the transcriptions; they are better learned by ear.)

   The phonetic transcriptions are enclosed in brackets, [ ]. Phonetic training is not necessary for students working with this book, however; the transcriptions are included as an aid for teachers, so that they can see at a glance the subject matter of each lesson. The students can work on the exercises with the sole help of the recording.

Spelling Some Portuguese words are pronounced differently according to their syntactic environment and speed of delivery; for instance, *não* 'do not' is often pronounced *num,* and *está* 'is' is usually pronounced *tá.* I have indicated this only for *está/tá. Não* will sometimes be pronounced *num* in the dialogues, but the spelling is *não* in all cases.

How to Use the Workbook

OVERVIEW

This workbook is not meant to be the exclusive basis of a course. It is not advisable to spend a long time working only on formal aspects of the language such as pronunciation. Rather, the material found here should be used in class as a complement to more traditional studies based on texts not planned around phonology. As a supplement, then, is the best way to make use of this workbook, and this is also the reason for minimal explanations. The purpose is not to teach Portuguese in toto but to perfect just one, if a very important, aspect of proficiency in the language.

WORKING WITHIN A TYPICAL SYLLABUS

The pronunciation workbook can be covered in about sixteen weeks (two lessons per week), taking up no more than fifteen to twenty minutes per class. Additional time will be spent self-teaching outside class with help of the recording. When working with the listening drills in class, the teacher should supplement the recording with his or her own pronunciation; this, besides lending liveliness to the class, has the advantage of exposing the students to differences in voice, style of pronunciation, and perhaps regional speech. It is also possible to work through the material by oneself, missing, of course, the advantages provided by the live interchange with the teacher and among the students (see below, Tips for the Self-Teaching Student).

The workbook can be used with beginning and intermediate students, along with a regular handbook, and with advanced students who need remedial work in pronunciation. It is highly desirable to work on pronunciation when first taking up the study of the language in order to avoid establishing poor pronunciation habits, which may prove difficult to eradicate afterward (the "fossilization" phenomenon, mentioned above). When working in class, the teacher can control the accuracy of the students' reproduction of the pronunciation models.

THE EXERCISES

I have devised four main types of exercises:

- *Isolated words and phrases* introduce each sound and sound sequence.
- *Sentences* help the development of fluency and the acquisition of intonation patterns.
- *Minimal pairs* help students who have trouble making phonological distinctions that are present in Portuguese but not in English.
- *Dialogues* provide examples of speech used in normal situations, with (almost) every difficulty occurring in the text as happens in real-life conversation.

How much time is spent on each type of exercise will depend on the needs and deficiencies of individual students. Beginning students should be exposed to the whole course, following the lessons in order. For remedial work a previous diagnosis is advisable.

Lessons 1–3 As mentioned above, exercises in the first three lessons are arranged into two stages to serve intermediate and advanced students as well as beginners. Those marked "For Advanced Students" include whole sentences and phrases and are planned for the use of students who already have some proficiency with the language but still need to work on pronunciation. Beginning students should skip over all exercises so marked.

Lessons 4–32 After Lesson 4, the distinction between exercises for beginning and advanced students is no longer maintained. All students can do all the exercises, regardless of their degree of fluency in the language.

THE IMPORTANCE OF REPETITION

Sentences and dialogues With the sentences and the dialogues the first step is to understand their meaning. There are many ways to achieve comprehension, and teachers will use the methods they prefer. Once a dialogue is properly understood, the student should listen to it several times to memorize the words and their pronunciation. The idea is to free the student both from the effort of deciphering the text and from the need to pronounce words seen for the first time. The student will thus be able to concentrate on pronunciation (including intonation) and expression, exactly as if learning a part in a play. In fact, the dialogues can be enacted as little dramas, thus adding interest to the study of pronunciation and encouraging the use of the language in communicatively natural situations. But the main function of the sentences and dialogues is for practicing comparatively long stretches of discourse, along with intonation and expression.

Drills The drills are comparable to scales and arpeggios in music: they are necessary, but they are only a part of the study of the language. Just as a music student must play compositions as well as scales, the language student must repeat drills to learn pronunciation, as well as practice pronunciation in guided and free conversation. Just as in music, the command of expression in language depends crucially on the acquisition of automatisms.

Studying with the CDs

For technical reasons it was not possible to include all instructions in the recording, nor every exercise on a separate track. Instructions for doing the exercises, along with locations of the exercises on the CDs, are given in the workbook.

For each exercise, reference is given in the workbook to the CD and track on which it is recorded; thus, for the first exercise in Lesson 1:

> CD1 – track 2

The recording of the exercise will be on track 2 of the first CD.

Students should locate the exercise on the CD, then look at the exercise in the workbook. The words and phrases are written out, along with instructions for doing the exercises. The instructions are numbered *a, b,* and *c.*

a. Listen.

This instruction is given in the workbook and in the recording. Students should do exactly as it says: listen to the recording. The speaker says the words, separated by pauses.

b. Listen again. Repeat aloud after each word.

This instruction is given in the workbook but not in the recording. Students should return to the beginning of track 2. This time they should listen to the words and repeat them in the pauses.

c. Read each word aloud.

This instruction is given only in the workbook. Students should repeat the words, remembering how they were pronounced in the recording.

Having several different drills for the same list of words allows for variations according to the needs of individual students. The teacher or the students themselves can evaluate what kinds of drills they need to spend time on.

Tips for the Self-Teaching Student

Although this book was planned as an aid to classroom work, it can also be used in self-teaching, by students who want to supplement their classes or their previously acquired knowledge of Portuguese with exercises leading to a better pronunciation of the language. Such students will depend on the recording. For them I have several pieces of advice.

Tip 1 Do not worry about the phonetic transcriptions. These are meant to orient the linguistically trained teacher (or student). They are not mandatory. If you are not proficient in phonetic symbols, feel free to disregard them. All the necessary information for correct pronunciation is on the CD.

Tip 2 I made every effort to provide easily understandable descriptions of each sound. But a sound cannot be adequately described in words, and I would suggest that you concentrate as much as possible on the models provided on the CD. You should also seize every opportunity to make verbal contact with native speakers. Brazilians are usually cheerful, talkative, and willing to criticize and correct their friends' pronunciation.

Tip 3 When working with the CD, monitor your own reproduction of the model pronunciation—if possible, by recording it and playing it back. Especially in the first stages, try to be rigorous and demanding in order to develop the automatisms that make up correct pronunciation. Making yourself understood is not enough! As you proceed, work on the production of longer and longer utterances—whole words, small phrases, sentences. Your aim should be to go through stretches of discourse fluently, without undue breaks or faulty intonation.

Tip 4 Do not be afraid of learning Portuguese sentences by rote—the more such sentences you have stored in your memory, the easier it will be to apply the same sounds, junctures, and intonation contours to your own utterances.

Tip 5 Finally, never work for a long time just on pronunciation. Rather, intersperse your pronunciation exercises with grammatical exercises and with lots of free conversation. In this way you will be able to develop good pronunciation of Portuguese—it is mainly a matter of patience and intelligent work.

TALKING BRAZILIAN

Lesson 1

Vowels [i, ə]; consonants [b, f, g, s, ʃ, v, z, ʒ] and [m, n]

(word-initial or after unstressed oral vowel)

For Beginning Students

CD1 — track 2

a. Listen.

fiz [ˈfiːs]	'(I) made / have made'	
xis [ˈʃiːs]	'x [letter]'	
giz [ˈʒiːs]	'chalk'	
bis [ˈbiːs]	'encore'	
vi [ˈviː]	'(I) have seen'	
se [siː]	'if'	
me [miː]	'me'	
xixi [ʃiˈʃiː]	'pee'	
Nini [niˈniː]	(woman's nickname)	
visa [ˈviːzə]	'visa'	
ficha [ˈfiːʃə]	'token'	
missa [ˈmiːsə]	'mass (religious)'	
Isa [ˈiːzə]	(woman's name)	

giga [ˈʒiːgə]	'jig'
na missa [nəˈmiːsə]	'at mass'
bife [ˈbiːfi]	'steak'
visse [ˈviːsi]	'(he/she) saw [subjunctive]'
Nice [ˈniːsi]	(woman's name)
figas [ˈfiːgəs]	'amulets'
bifes [ˈbiːfis]	'steaks'
fichas [ˈfiːʃəs]	'tokens'
missas [ˈmiːsəs]	'masses'
fisga [ˈfiːzgə]	'(he/she) hooks'
cisma [ˈsiːzmə]	'obsession'
cisne [ˈsiːzni]	'swan'

> ✿ Observe that **s** is always pronounced [z] when preceding a voiced consonant; thus, in Portuguese we never find sequences of, say, [sm] or [sl], as in English *smile, sleep*.

b. Listen again. Repeat aloud after each word.

c. Read each word aloud.

> ✿ All sounds introduced in this lesson are common to English and Portuguese.
>
> The vowel [i] occurs in *see,* and [ə] is the weak sound heard at the end of *cobra*. The vowel [ə] is written **a** and is always unstressed. It occurs in post-stress syllables: either at the end of a word, with or without a following **s** (*ficha, fichas*), or in the next-to-last syllable, when the syllable is unstressed (*bêbado*).
>
> Observe that a final unstressed [i] is normally written **e** and pronounced very short. When not final, it is written **i** or, very frequently, **e**—as in *perigo* 'danger,' normally pronounced [piˈriːgu]. When stressed, it is always written **i**, and then it is long, like all stressed vowels in Portuguese.
>
> The consonants studied in this lesson occur in English words as follows: [b] (written **b**) as in _bee;_ [f] (written **f**) as in _fee;_ [g] (written **g**) as in _go;_ [s] (written in several ways, for example, **s, c, ç, x,** final **z,** and several combinations) as in _see;_ [ʃ] (written **ch, x**) as in _she;_ [v] (written **v**) as in _violin;_ [z] (written **z, s, x**) as in _zoo;_ [ʒ] (written **g, j**) as in _usual._ The consonants [m] (written **m**) and [n] (written **n**), are identical to English **m** in *my* and **n** in *no,* respectively, when they

occur before a vowel (see Lessons 16–20 for their pronunciation when word-final or before a consonant).

For Advanced Students

CD1 — track 3

d. Listen.

Vi a ficha na mesa.	'I saw the token on the table.'
Cadê o giz?	'Where is the chalk?'
Isa está na missa	'Isa is at mass.'
Nice fez um bife.	'Nice cooked a steak.'

e. Listen again. Repeat aloud after each sentence.

f. Read each sentence aloud.

Cadê o giz?

Lesson 2

Final [ˈiːjə]

> 🖉 The final sequence [ˈiːjə], written **-ia,** sounds very close to **-ea** in English *idea.*

For Beginning Students

CD1 — track 4

a. Listen.

ia [ˈiːjə]	'(he/she) went'
via [ˈviːjə]	'(he/she) saw'
Bia [ˈbiːjə]	(woman's nickname)
chia [ˈʃiːjə]	'(he/she) squeaks'
mexia [miˈʃiːjə]	'(he/she) dealt with'
mia [ˈmiːjə]	'(he/she) meows'
guias [ˈgiːjəs]	'guides'

b. Listen again. Repeat aloud after each word.

c. Read each word aloud.

4

For Advanced Students

CD1—track 5

d. Listen.

Bia ia à Bahia.	'Bia went to Bahia.'
Bia mexia na pia.	'Bia was busy at the sink.'
O gato mia, o rato chia.	'The cat meows; the rat squeaks.'
Nini via o cisne.	'Nini saw the swan.'

e. Listen again. Repeat aloud after each sentence.

f. Read each sentence aloud.

Bia ia à Bahia

Lesson 3

Consonants [tʃ, dʒ]

The consonants [tʃ] and [dʒ] have identical counterparts in English: [tʃ] (written **t**) is pronounced like *ch* in English <u>*cheese,*</u> and [dʒ] (written **d**) like *j* in *jeans*. In Portuguese, they occur almost exclusively before the sounds [i] or [j] (written **i** or **e**), where they regularly replace [t] and [d], which never occur before [i]. One also finds [tʃ] and [dʒ] before other vowels when, in rapid speech, an [i] or a [j] is omitted, for example, in *mídia,* which is pronounced [ˈmiːdʒiə] in careful speech, but [ˈmiːdʒə] in fluent, relaxed speech.

For Beginning Students

CD1 — track 6

a. Listen.

te [tʃi]	'you [object]'
de [dʒi]	'of'
tia [ˈtʃiːjə]	'aunt'
dia [ˈdʒiːjə]	'day'

6

diga ['dʒiːgə]	'say [imperative]'
disse ['dʒiːsi]	'(he/she) said'
tive ['tʃiːvi]	'(I) had'
cite ['siːtʃi]	'mention [imperative]'
mídia ['miːdʒə]	'media'
Fídias ['fiːdʒəs]	(man's name)
vestia [visˈtʃiːjə]	'(he/she) got dressed'
as tias [əsˈtʃiːjəs]	'the aunts'

b. Listen again. Repeat aloud after each word.

c. Read each word aloud.

For Advanced Students

CD1 — track 7

d. Listen.

um dia de chuva	'a rainy day'
A tia se vestia de chita.	'The aunt wore calico.'
Eu tive um dia difícil.	'I have had a hard day.'
Vamos dividir esse bife?	'How about sharing this steak?'

e. Listen again. Repeat aloud after each sentence.

f. Read each sentence aloud.

Vamos dividir esse bife?

Lesson 4

Vowel [u]; semivowel [w]

The vowel [u] is close, but not identical, to **oo** in English *too*. Portuguese [u] is pronounced like Spanish or German **u,** that is, with a more energetic rounding of the lips and retraction of the tongue toward the back of the mouth than with English **oo.** A common mistake is to pronounce **u** with a **y**-glide, [ju], as in *use;* Portuguese **u** is a simple vowel. The student should listen carefully to the recording, then attempt to imitate the Portuguese sound. The vowel [u] is written **u;** when unstressed and at the end of a word, it is written **o** (whether or not it is followed by **s**). In many cases a nonfinal unstressed **o** is pronounced [u].

The semivowel [w] is virtually identical in the two languages. Its distribution, however, is different, and the student should pay attention to its environments. In Portuguese, for instance, there is a difference between [u] and [uw], so *nu* ['nuː] 'naked' does not rhyme with *sul* ['suːw] 'south.' Exercises on the opposition [u] / [uw] will be found in Lesson 11.

One more note on [w]: it is often written **l**—this being the normal pronunciation of the letter **l** when syllable-final.

CD1—track 8

a. **Listen.**

nu ['nuː]	'naked'
xuxu [ʃu'ʃuː]	'chayote squash'

chuva [ˈʃuːvə]	'rain'
chute [ˈʃuːtʃi]	'kick'
Xuxa [ˈʃuːʃə]	(woman's nickname)
isso [ˈiːsu]	'this'
sujo [ˈsuːʒu]	'dirty'
subo [ˈsuːbu]	'(I) go up'
musgo [ˈmuːzgu]	'moss'
viu [ˈviːw]	'(he/she) saw / has seen'
Gil [ˈʒiːw]	(man's name)
mil [ˈmiːw]	'one thousand'
subiu [suˈbiːw]	'(he/she) went up, climbed'
sua [ˈsuːwə]	'your'
nua [ˈnuːwə]	'naked [feminine]'
difícil [dʒiˈfiːsiw]	'difficult'
no guia [nuˈgiːjə]	'in the guidebook'
o musgo [uˈmuːzgu]	'the moss'
o chute [uˈʃuːtʃi]	'the kick'

b. Listen again. Repeat aloud after each word.

c. Read each word aloud.

CD1 — track 9

d. Listen.

Vi a figa.	'(I) have seen the amulet.'
Te vi na missa.	'(I) saw you at mass.'
mil figas	'one thousand amulets'
Isa viu mil figas.	'Isa saw one thousand amulets.'
Nini viu sua tia nua.	'Nini saw your aunt naked.'
o musgo sujo	'the dirty moss'

Bia mexia no musgo sujo.   'Bia was messing around with the dirty moss.'

Nini viu sua tia nua

e. Listen again. Repeat aloud after each sentence.

f. Read each sentence aloud.

Lesson 5

Vowel [ɛ]

The vowel [ɛ], written **e** or **é,** is practically identical to English **e** in **pet**—but, like all vowels, it is pronounced long when stressed.

CD1—track 10

a. Listen.

és [ˈɛːs]	'(you) are'
é [ˈɛː]	'(he/she) is / (you) are'
fé [ˈfɛː]	'faith'
Zé [ˈzɛː]	(man's nickname)
José [ʒuˈzɛː]	(man's name)
Tibé [tʃiˈbɛː]	'Tibet'
mel [ˈmɛːw]	'honey'
céu [ˈsɛːw]	'sky'
véu [ˈvɛːw]	'veil'
chefe [ˈʃɛːfi]	'boss'
Eva [ˈɛːvə]	(woman's name)

bebe ['bɛːbi]   '(he/she) drinks'
nega ['neːgə]   '(he/she) denies'

b. Listen again. Repeat aloud after each word.

c. Read each word aloud.

CD1—track 11

d. Listen.

Isso é mel.   'This is honey.'
O véu é sujo.   'The veil is dirty.'
Isso é difícil.   'This is difficult.'
Eva é sua tia.   'Eva is your aunt.'
O chefe viu José na chuva.   'The boss saw José in the rain.'

Isso é difícil

🎧 Starting with this lesson, the student should pay special attention to vowel reduction at word boundaries. For instance, in the sentence *Eva é sua tia,* given above, the final -**a** of *Eva,* being unstressed and before a word beginning with a vowel, is usually reduced. In normal speech, it becomes a semivowel [ə], so that the sequence -**va é** is pronounced as a single syllable; in rapid speech, the final -**a** of *Eva* is omitted, so the sentence sounds like [ˈɛːvɛˈsuːwəˈtʃiːjə]. Vowel reduction is a widespread phenomenon, and it is amply exemplified in the coming lessons; the rules of vowel reduction and omission are given in full in *Modern Portuguese,* 5.1.1.

e. Listen again. Repeat aloud after each sentence.

f. Read each sentence aloud.

Lesson 6

Vowel [a]

♪ The sound of Portuguese [a] (written **a** or **á**) is close to the sound of **o** in *object* (American pronunciation), but longer, particularly when stressed. It is identical to Spanish **á** in *más* and French **a** in *las*. Portuguese [a] is also close to English **a** in *father*, but the latter is usually pronounced with a noticeable retraction of the body of the tongue toward the back of the mouth; this retraction is absent from the Portuguese pronunciation.

CD1 — track 12

a. Listen.

faz ['faːs]	'(he/she) makes'
más ['maːs]	'bad [feminine plural]'
babá [ba'baː]	'babysitter'
jabá [ʒa'baː]	'jerked meat'
chá ['ʃaː]	'tea'
chave ['ʃaːvi]	'key'
assa ['aːsə]	'(he/she) bakes'
água ['aːgwə]	'water'
diabo [dʒi'aːbu]	'devil'

15

Tiago [tʃi'aːgu]	(man's name)
faixas ['faːʃəs]	'bandages'
asma ['aːzmə]	'asthma'
asno ['aːznu]	'burro'
anel [a'nɛːw]	'ring (jewelry)'
azul [a'zuːw]	'blue'
Bahia [ba'iːjə]	'Bahia'

b. Listen again. Repeat aloud after each word.

c. Read each word aloud.

Tiago viu a chave

CD1 — track 13

d. Listen.

Tiago viu a chave.	'Tiago saw the key.'
A Bia é a babá da sua tia.	'Bia is your aunt's babysitter.'
A faixa é azul.	'The band is blue.'
Zé faz o chá.	'Zé makes the tea.'

e. Listen again. Repeat aloud after each sentence.

f. Read each sentence aloud.

Lesson 7

Semivowel [j]

> 🎧 This semivowel is identical to English **y** in *day*. It is very frequent at the ends of words and syllables and between vowels, but not at the beginnings of words.

CD1—track 14

a. Listen.

vai [ˈvaːj]	'(he/she) goes'
sai [ˈsaːj]	'(he/she) goes out'
fui [ˈfuːj]	'(I) have gone'
azuis [aˈzuːjs]	'blue [plural]'
anéis [aˈnɛːjs]	'rings'
sais [ˈsaːjs]	'salts'
saia [ˈsaːjə]	'skirt'
vaia [ˈvaːjə]	'booing'
fio [ˈfiːju]	'cord'
chio [ˈʃiːju]	'(I) squeak'

b. **Listen again. Repeat aloud after each word.**

c. **Read each word aloud.**

CD1 — track 15

d. **Listen.**

Tiago vai à Bahia.	'Tiago goes to Bahia.'
as saias azuis de Nini	'Nini's blue skirts'
Fui à Bahia e vi os anéis.	'(I) went to Bahia and saw the rings.'
José mexia no fio.	'José messed around with the cord.'

As saias azuis de Nini

e. **Listen again. Repeat aloud after each sentence.**

f. **Read each sentence aloud.**

Lesson 8

Consonants [p, t, k]

The Portuguese sounds [p], [t], and [k] (written **p; t;** and **c** or **q,** respectively) lack the aspiration found in English *pie, key, too*. In the English words there is a perceptible puff of air between the consonant and the following vowel; in the Portuguese words *pai* 'father,' *que* 'which,' and *tu* 'you' the vowel immediately follows the consonant, without aspiration. Portuguese is, in this respect, similar to French, Spanish, and Italian. The student must try to reproduce the models, avoiding the aspiration.

Furthermore, [t] (and [d] as well) is pronounced with the tongue tip in a slightly more forward position in Portuguese than in English. When saying the English word *too,* the tongue tip touches the upper gums just above the teeth; but for Portuguese *tu* 'you' the tongue comes into contact with the teeth and lies in a flatter position against the gums.

CD1—track 16

a. Listen.

festa [ˈfɛːstə]	'party'	
casca [ˈkaːskə]	'peel, shell'	
isca [ˈiːskə]	'bait'	

20

caspa [ˈkaːspə]	'dandruff'
USP [ˈuːspi]	'USP (University of São Paulo)'
está [isˈtaː]	'(he/she) is'
esquece [isˈkɛːsi]	'(he/she) forgets'
mosquito [musˈkiːtu]	'mosquito'
espécie [isˈpɛːsi]	'species'
até [aˈtɛː]	'until'
a pé [aˈpɛː]	'on foot'
fatal [faˈtaːw]	'fatal'
pai [ˈpaːj]	'father'
paz [ˈpaːs]	'peace'
tá [ˈtaː]	'OK'
tudo [ˈtuːdu]	'everything'
quieto [ˈkɛːtu]	'still, quiet'
quis [ˈkiːs]	'(he/she) wanted'
cubo [ˈkuːbu]	'cube'
descasque [dʒisˈkaːski]	'(he/she) peels [subjunctive]'
na festa [nəˈfɛːstə]	'at the party'

b. Listen again. Repeat aloud after each word.

c. Read each word aloud.

CD1 — track 17

d. Listen.

Esse mosquito é chato.	'This mosquito is a nuisance.'
Fui a pé daqui até a USP.	'I went on foot from here to USP.'
A festa é nessa casa.	'The party is at this house.'
Tudo está quieto.	'All is quiet.'
O pai quis chá.	'The father wanted some tea.'

Esse mosquito é chato

e. Listen again. Repeat aloud after each sentence.

f. Read each sentence aloud.

Lesson 9

Vowel [ɔ]

🖋 Portuguese [ɔ] (written **o** or **ó**) sounds like English **a** in *wall*—it is a low vowel pronounced with rounded lips. It also occurs in *flaw* in the General American or British pronunciation: [ˈflɔː]. However, many people in the American Midwest pronounce it [ˈflɒː], without rounding. Portuguese [ɔ] is always rounded.

CD1 — track 18

a. Listen.

voz [ˈvɔːs]	'voice'	
foz [ˈfɔːs]	'mouth (of a river)'	
avós [aˈvɔːs]	'grandparents'	
só [ˈsɔː]	'alone'	
avó [aˈvɔː]	'grandmother'	
nó [nɔː]	'knot'	
Jacó [ʒaˈkɔː]	(man's name)	
vovó [vɔˈvɔː]	'grandma'	
choque [ˈʃɔːki]	'shock'	
gosto [ˈgɔːstu]	'(I) like'	

boto ['bɔːtu]	'(I) put'
sobe ['sɔːbi]	'(he/she) goes up, climbs'
nova ['nɔːvə]	'new [feminine]'
joga ['ʒɔːgə]	'(he/she) plays'

🖋 Special attention must be paid to the pronunciation of the diphthong [ɔw] (always written **ol**).

---

sol ['sɔːw]	'sun'
futebol [futʃi'bɔw]	'soccer'
volto ['vɔːwtu]	'(I) come back'
solta ['sɔːwtə]	'(he/she) releases / lets go'

b. Listen again. Repeat aloud after each word.

c. Read each word aloud.

CD1—track 19

d. Listen.

Gosto da sua voz.	'(I) like your voice.'
O Jacó joga futebol.	'Jacó plays soccer.'
Só a vovó gosta de sol.	'Only grandma enjoys the sunlight.'
Vovó subiu a pé até a casa nova.	'Grandma went to the new house on foot.'
Bia volta às sete.	'Bia is coming back at seven.'

e. Listen again. Repeat aloud after each sentence.

f. Read each sentence aloud.

CD1—track 20

g. Listen, then check the word you have heard: the one with [a] or the one with [ɔ].

Só a vovó gosta de sol

[a]

- [ ] *Sá* (surname)
- [ ] *pá* 'shovel'
- [ ] *bala* 'bullet'
- [ ] *gasta* '(he/she) spends'
- [ ] *carta* 'letter'
- [ ] *mata* 'forest'

[ɔ]

- [ ] *só* 'alone'
- [ ] *pó* 'dust'
- [ ] *bola* 'ball'
- [ ] *gosta* '(he/she) likes'
- [ ] *corta* '(he/she) cuts'
- [ ] *Mota* (surname)

☞ **Check your answers with the Key.**

Lesson 10

Consonants [d, l, h]

🎧 On the pronunciation of Portuguese [d], see Lesson 8 on the pronunciation of [t].

The sound [l] is very close to that of English **l** in *low.* But the letter **l** is pronounced differently when syllable-final; see Lesson 4.

About [h], written **r** or **rr,** some reminders are in order (see *Modern Portuguese* 2.2 for more details):

1. This sound is usually omitted when at the end of a verb form: *ficar* [fi'kaː], *quer* ['kɛː]. In the transcriptions I always include it.
2. The pronunciation [h] is the most common pronunciation in Brazil for **rr** or syllable-final **r.** But other pronunciations are accepted as correct: [r], [x], etc.
3. The sound [h] is normally semi-voiced, like **h** in English *ahead,* except when final or before a voiceless consonant.

CD1 — track 21

a. Listen.

dez ['dɛːs]   'ten'
duas ['duːwəs]   'two [feminine]'

dó ['dɔː]	'pity'	
dado ['daːdu]	'die (for games)'	

lá ['laː]	'there'
Lia ['liːjə]	(woman's name)
luz ['luːs]	'light'
leve ['lɛːvi]	'lightweight'
sala ['saːlə]	'living room'

rato ['haːtu]	'rat'
régua ['hɛːgwə]	'ruler'
ri ['hiː]	'(he/she) laughs'
rói ['hɔːj]	'(he/she) gnaws'

carro ['kaːhu]	'car'
berra ['bɛːhə]	'(he/she) yells'
burro ['buːhu]	'donkey'

mar ['maːh]	'sea'
flor ['floːh]	'flower'
menor [me'nɔːh]	'smaller'
maior [ma'jɔːh]	'bigger'
Artur [ah'tuːh]	(man's name)

placa ['plaːkə]	'plate'
flauta ['flaːwtə]	'flute'
blusa ['bluːzə]	'blouse'
glacial [glasi'aːw]	'glacial'
ciclo ['siːklu]	'cycle'

b. Listen again. Repeat aloud after each word.

c. Read each word aloud.

CD1 — track 22

d. Listen.

Papai quer dez faixas.	'Daddy wants ten bands.'
O rato rói só a casca.	'The rat gnaws only the shell.'
O carro do Artur é azul.	'Artur's car is blue.'
O dado está lá na sala.	'The die is in the living room.'
Artur quer ficar na sala.	'Artur wants to stay in the living room.'
Sua amiga toca flauta.	'Your friend plays the flute.'
Sua blusa é azul.	'Your blouse is blue.'
Aquela placa é maior do que essa.	'That plate is bigger than this one.'

O carro do Artur é azul

e. Listen again. Repeat aloud after each sentence.

f. Read each sentence aloud.

Lesson 11

Semivowel [w] (again)

📌 The examples in this lesson are planned to develop the student's ability to distinguish between the vowel [u] and the sequence [uw] (written **ul**), which are often confused by speakers of English but must be differentiated.

CD1 — track 23

a. Listen.

nu [ˈnuː]		'naked'
sul [ˈsuːw]		'south'
Itu [iˈtuː]		(name of a city)
azul [aˈzuːw]		'blue'
fuga [ˈfuːɡə]		'flight'
pulga [ˈpuːwɡə]		'flea'
luta [ˈluːtə]		'struggle'
multa [ˈmuːwtə]		'fine (penalty)'
chuto [ˈʃuːtu]		'(I) kick'
culto [ˈkuːwtu]		'cult'

lupa ['luːpə]	'magnifying glass'
culpa ['kuːwpə]	'guilt'
suco ['suːku]	'juice'
sulco ['suːwku]	'furrow, groove'
sugava [su'gaːvə]	'(he/she) sucked'
julgava [ʒuw'gaːvə]	'(he/she) judged'
lugar [lu'gaːh]	'place'
vulgar [vuw'gaːh]	'vulgar'
fugia [fu'ʒiːjə]	'(he/she) fled'
fulgia [fuw'ʒiːjə]	'(he/she) shone'

b. Listen again. Repeat aloud after each word.

c. Read each word aloud.

O juiz chutava a bola

CD1 — track 24

d. Listen.

Me dá a lupa azul.	'Give me the blue magnifying glass.'
O juiz chutava a bola.	'The referee kicked the ball.'
O juiz multava o clube.	'The referee fined the club.'
Joga o suco no sulco.	'Pour the juice into the groove.'
Lia vive ao sul de Itu.	'Lia lives south of Itu.'

e. Listen again. Repeat aloud after each sentence.

f. Read each sentence aloud.

Lesson 12

Vowel [e]; diphthong [ej]

In English, the sound of Portuguese [e] (written **e** or **ê**) occurs as part of a diphthong, never alone. Take the word *day:* after the [d] sound we have [e], immediately followed by a **y**-glide, [j]. To produce Portuguese [e], you must pronounce the vowel in *day,* but stop short of pronouncing the glide. The result is identical to French **é** in *chanté.*

The main difficulty here is keeping [e] and [ɛ] apart, since there are pairs of words distinguished only on the basis of this difference: *sede* ['seːdʒi] 'thirst' versus *sede* ['sɛːdʒi] 'headquarters'; *pê* ['peː] 'p (letter)' versus *pé* ['pɛː] 'foot.' The problem is both phonological (because English does not contain this opposition) and orthographic (because both sounds may be represented by **e**). The student should pay attention to this point to avoid confusing [e] and [ɛ] and to avoid confusing [e] and the diphthong [ej].

The diphthong [ej] (written **ei**) is identical to English **ay** in *day.*

CD1—track 25

a. Listen.

[e / ej]

sei ['seːj]   '(I) know'

32

cê ['seː]	'c (letter)'
lei ['leːj]	'law'
lê ['leː]	'(he/she) reads'
dei ['deːj]	'(I) gave'
dê ['deː]	'give [imperative]'

peguei [pe'geːj]	'(I) have caught'
ipê [i'peː]	'ipê (tree)'

reis ['heːjs]	'kings'
rês ['heːs]	'head of cattle'

deita ['deːjtə]	'(he/she) lies down'
eta ['eːtə]	'oops!'
gelo ['ʒeːlu]	'ice'
ei-lo ['eːjlu]	'here it is'
peito ['peːjtu]	'chest (of a person)'
gueto ['geːtu]	'ghetto'

feia ['feːjə]	'ugly [feminine]'
meio ['meːju]	'half'

blefe ['bleːfi]	'bluff'
chego ['ʃeːgu]	'(I) arrive'
medo ['meːdu]	'fear'
erro ['eːhu]	'mistake'

[e / ɛ]

cê ['seː]	'c (letter)'
sé ['sɛː]	'cathedral'
zê ['zeː]	'z (letter)'
Zé ['zɛː]	(man's nickname)
sede ['seːdʒi]	'thirst'
sede ['sɛːdʒi]	'headquarters'
pelo ['peːlu]	'fur'
pelo ['pɛːlu]	'(I) peel'
queijo ['keːʒu]	'cheese'

[ej / ɛj]

leia [ˈleːjə]	'read [imperative]'
Léa [ˈlɛːjə]	(woman's name)
reis [ˈheːjs]	'kings'
réis [ˈhɛːjs]	'reis (old Brazilian coin)'
as leis [azˈleːjs]	'the laws'
anéis [aˈnɛːjs]	'rings'

[ew / ɛw]

seu [ˈseːw]	'his/her; your'
céu [ˈsɛːw]	'sky'
meu [ˈmeːw]	'my'
mel [ˈmɛːw]	'honey'
bateu [baˈteːw]	'(he/she) spanked'
chapéu [ʃaˈpɛːw]	'hat'
Manuel [manuˈɛːw]	(man's name)
acelga [aˈsɛːwgə]	'chard'
móvel [ˈmɔːvew]	'chest of drawers'
amável [aˈmaːvew]	'kind (nice)'

b. Listen again. Repeat aloud after each word.

c. Read each word aloud.

CD1—track 26

d. Listen.

Me dê um cubo de gelo.	'Give me an ice cube.'
Peguei a bola no peito.	'I caught the ball on (my) chest.'
Essa blusa é meio feia.	'This blouse is kind of ugly.'
O rei respeita a lei.	'The king abides by the law.'
Zé fala mal de você.	'Zé talks trash about you.'
Achei sete queijos.	'(I) found seven cheeses.'
de três a dez quilos	'from three to ten kilos'

A Léa bateu no Manuel.	'Léa hit Manuel.'
Leia isso aí.	'Read this.'
Léa é feia.	'Léa is ugly.'
Eu gosto do Manuel.	'I like Manuel.'
O céu é azul.	'The sky is blue.'
Peguei meu chapéu no móvel.	'I took my hat from the chest of drawers.'

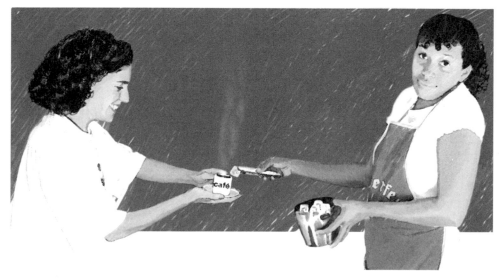

Me dê um cubo de gelo

e. Listen again. Repeat aloud after each sentence.

f. Read each sentence aloud.

CD1—track 27

g. Listen, then check the word you have heard: the one with [e] or the one with [ɛ].

[e]	[ɛ]
☐ *Fê* (nickname)	☐ *fé* 'faith'
☐ *cê* 'c (letter)'	☐ *sé* 'cathedral'

□ *meu* 'my'   □ *mel* 'honey'
□ *seu* 'your'   □ *céu* 'sky'
□ *sede* 'thirst'   □ *sede* 'seat (of government)'

CD1—track 28

---

h. Listen, then check the word you have heard: the one with [e] or the one with [ej].

[e]   [ej]

□ *lê* '(he/she) reads'   □ *lei* 'law'
□ *cê* 'c (letter)'   □ *sei* '(I) know'
□ *dê* 'give'   □ *dei* '(I) gave'
□ *rolê* 'turtleneck'   □ *rolei* '(I) rolled over'

⊶ **Check your answers with the Key.**

Lesson 13

Vowel [o]; diphthong [ow]

In English, the sound of Portuguese [o] (written **o** or **ô**) occurs only as the first part of a diphthong—for example, in the word *no*. Portuguese [o] sounds like the first part of the English diphthong; it is made with a more definite rounding of the lips than is usual when the English sound is made. The Portuguese [o] is identical to French **eau** in *beau*.

The diphthong [ow] is similar to English **o** in *no* (always pronounced with rounded lips). It is written **ol**—not **ou**, which stands for [o] in the speech of almost all Brazilian speakers.

CD1—track 29

a. Listen.

[o / ɔ]

avô [aˈvoː]	'grandfather'
avó [aˈvɔː]	'grandmother'
dou [doː]	'(I) give'
dó [dɔː]	'pity'
sou [soː]	'(I) am'
só [sɔː]	'only'

37

toco ['toːku]	'tree stump'
toco ['tɔːku]	'(I) play'
touca ['toːkə]	'bathing cap'
toca ['tɔːkə]	'(he/she) plays'
vovô [vo'voː]	'grandpa'
vovó [vɔ'vɔː]	'grandma'
cortou [koh'toː]	'(he/she) cut [past]'
bolota [bɔ'lɔːtə]	'acorn'
colosso [ko'loːsu]	'great amount'

[o / ow]

> ✍ English speakers have some difficulty in distinguishing [o] from [ow] (written **ol**) because the opposition does not exist in English.

coxa ['koːʃə]	'thigh'
colcha ['koːwʃə]	'bedspread'
popa ['poːpə]	'stern (of a boat)'
polpa ['poːwpə]	'pulp'
votei [vo'teːj]	'(I) voted'
voltei [vow'teːj]	'(I) came back'
ligou [li'goː]	'(he/she) phoned'
gol ['goːw]	'goal (in soccer)'

[oj / ɔj]

> ✍ The diphthong [ɔj] presents no difficulty, being identical to English **oy** in *boy*. But the student should be careful in distinguishing it from [oj], which has no English counterpart.

dois ['doːjs]	'two'
dói ['dɔːj]	'(it) hurts'
apoio [a'poːju]	'support'
apóio [a'pɔːju]	'(I) support'
boi ['boːj]	'ox'
rói ['hɔːj]	'(he/she) gnaws'

goiaba [goˈjaːbə]   'guava'
jóia [ˈʒɔːjə]   'jewel'

[ow / ɔw]

gol [ˈgoːw]   'goal (in soccer)'
sol [ˈsɔːw]   'sun'
polpa [ˈpoːwpə]   'pulp'
solta [ˈsɔːwtə]   '(he/she) releases, lets go'

b. Listen again. Repeat aloud after each word.

c. Read each word aloud.

CD1—track 30

d. Listen.

Volta logo!	'Come back soon!'
Seu avô está ótimo.	'Your grandfather is in good shape.'
Eu apóio esse sujeito.	'I am for that guy.'
Vou voltar a votar nesse partido.	'(I) am going to vote for that party again.'
Vovô fez dois gols no jogo.	'Grandpa scored two goals in the game.'
Hoje o sol tá terrível.	'The sun is terrible today.'

e. Listen again. Repeat aloud after each sentence.

f. Read each sentence aloud.

CD1—track 31

g. Listen, then check the word you have heard: the one with [o] or the one with [ɔ].

Hoje o sol tá terrível

[o]	[ɔ]
☐ *dou* '(I) give'	☐ *dó* 'pity'
☐ *sou* '(I) am'	☐ *só* 'only'
☐ *avô* 'grandfather'	☐ *avó* 'grandmother'
☐ *corte* '(royal) court'	☐ *corte* 'cut'
☐ *solto* 'free'	☐ *solto* '(I) let loose'

Check your answers with the Key.

CD1 — track 32

h. Listen, then check the word you have heard: the one with [o] or the one with [ow].

[o]

- □ *xô* 'shoo!'
- □ *popa* 'stern (of a boat)'
- □ *coxa* 'thigh'
- □ *votei* '(I) voted'

[ow]

- □ *show* 'show'
- □ *polpa* 'pulp'
- □ *colcha* 'bedspread'
- □ *voltei* '(I) came back'

☞ **Check your answers with the Key.**

Lesson 14

Consonant [ɾ]

♫ The consonant [ɾ] (written **r**) has the sound of **t** in *auto,* **dd** in *ladder* (American pronunciation). This sound is identical to that of Spanish **r** in *cara.* It occurs between vowels and after a consonant in the clusters [bɾ, dɾ, fɾ, gɾ, kɾ, pɾ, tɾ, vɾ], written **br, dr, fr, gr, cr, pr, tr,** and **vr,** respectively. It never occurs word-initially nor (in the variety of Portuguese here described) at the end of a syllable.

Word-final **r** is pronounced [h] (or a variant of [h]; see Lesson 10). But when a word ends with **r** and is followed without pause by a word beginning with a vowel, the **r** is pronounced [ɾ], as if it were between vowels in a word; for example, *amor eterno* 'eternal love' is pronounced as one word, *amoreterno* [aˌmoɾɛˈtɛhnu]. No [ɾ] appears when the first word is a verb, however, because a final **r** is usually silent in such cases: *ser amigo* 'to be a friend' is normally pronounced [ˌseːaˈmiːgu] in fluent speech; see *Modern Portuguese* 2.2 for details.

CD1—track 33

a. Listen.

fora [ˈfɔːɾə]	'outside'
vara [ˈvaːɾə]	'rod'
mares [ˈmaːɾis]	'seas'

muro ['muːɾu]	'wall'	
garoa [ga'ɾoːwə]	'drizzle'	
tirou [tʃi'ɾoː]	'(he/she) took away'	
parede [pa'ɾeːdʒi]	'wall'	
farol [fa'ɾɔːw]	'headlight'	

bravo ['bɾaːvu]	'wild'	
cravo ['kɾaːvu]	'carnation'	
frio ['fɾiːju]	'cold'	
três ['tɾeːjs]	'three'	
prova ['pɾɔːvə]	'proof'	
livro ['liːvɾu]	'book'	
sobra ['sɔːbɾə]	'leftover'	

[h] BECOMES [ɾ] BEFORE A WORD BEGINNING WITH A VOWEL

amor [a'moːh]	'love'	
amor eterno [aˌmoːɾɛ'tɛːhnu]	'eternal love'	
bar ['baːh]	'pub'	
bar aberto [ˌbaːɾa'bɛːhtu]	'open bar'	
Artur [ah'tuːh]	(man's name)	
Artur Azevedo [ahˌtuːɾaze'veːdu]	(his *full* name)	

b. Listen again. Repeat aloud after each word or phrase.

c. Read each word or phrase aloud.

CD1—track 34

d. Listen.

Ela jurou amor eterno.	'She swore eternal love.'
A garoa me irrita.	'The drizzle irritates me.'
Artur Azevedo escrevia livros de poesia.	'Artur Azevedo wrote poetry books.'
O mar é azul ou verde.	'The sea is either blue or green.'

O mar é azul ou verde

e. Listen again. Repeat aloud after each sentence.

f. Read each sentence aloud.

Lesson 15

Consonant [ʎ]

🎧 The consonant [ʎ] (written **lh** or **li**) has no exact correlate in English. It is pronounced like **gli** in Italian *paglia;* that is, it is a palatal lateral consonant. As in other languages, this sound tends to become [j] (as in English *yes*), but the process is much less advanced in Portuguese than in Spanish, so pronunciations like *paia* [ˈpaːjə] for *palha* 'straw' are frowned upon as uncultured.

The sounds [l] and [ʎ] are pronounced differently. For [l] one puts the tip of the tongue against the gums or the upper teeth, keeping the body of the tongue low; for [ʎ] one raises the body of the tongue, placing it against the palate (mainly the front part) while lowering the tip, which is usually placed behind the lower teeth. This consonant occurs in Portuguese almost exclusively between vowels, and word-initially only in a few loanwords, like *lhama* 'llama,' and in the clitic *lhe*.

CD1 — track 35

a. Listen.

milho [ˈmiːʎu]	'corn (grain)'
falha [ˈfaːʎə]	'fault (blame)'
olha [ˈɔːʎə]	'look [imperative]'
bolha [ˈboːʎə]	'bubble'

45

ilha [ˈiːʎə]	'island'	
agulha [agˈuːʎə]	'needle'	
olhava [oˈʎaːvə]	'(he/she) looked'	
mulher [muˈʎɛːh]	'woman'	
molhou [moˈʎoː]	'(he/she) moistened'	
melhor [mɛˈʎɔːh]	'better'	
falhou [faˈʎoː]	'(he/she) failed'	

In normal Brazilian pronunciation, the endings **-lio, -lia,** when unstressed, are also pronounced with a [ʎ], as in the examples below.

Júlio [ˈʒuːʎu]	(man's name)
julho [ˈʒuːʎu]	'July' [same pronunciation as *Júlio*]
famíia [faˈmiːʎə]	'family'
dália [ˈdaːʎə]	'dahlia'

b. Listen again. Repeat aloud after each word.

c. Read each word aloud.

CD1—track 36

d. Listen.

Olha o joelho do Júlio!	'Look at Júlio's knee!'
Marajó é a maior ilha do Brasil.	'Marajó is the largest island in Brazil.'
Sua família gosta de broa de milho.	'Your family enjoys corn bread.'
Eu colho as dálias em julho.	'I pick the dahlias in July.'

e. Listen again. Repeat aloud after each sentence.

f. Read each sentence aloud.

CD1—track 37

g. Listen, then check the word you have heard: the one with [ʎ] or the one with [l].

[ʎ]

- □ *falha* 'fault'
- □ *velha* 'old [feminine]'
- □ *rolha* 'cork'
- □ *filha* 'daughter'
- □ *molha* '(he/she) moistens'
- □ *pulha* 'scoundrel'

[l]

- □ *fala* 'speech'
- □ *vela* 'sail'
- □ *rola* 'dove (bird)'
- □ *fila* 'line (of people)'
- □ *mola* 'spring (in a mechanism)'
- □ *pula* '(he/she) jumps'

☛ **Check your answers with the Key.**

CD1—track 38

h. Listen, then check the word you have heard: the one with [ʎ] or the one with [li].

[ʎ]

- □ *alhado* 'full of garlic'
- □ *afilhado* 'godson'
- □ *olhava* '(he/she) looked'
- □ *ralhava* '(he/she) scolded'

[li]

- □ *aliado* 'ally'
- □ *afiliado* 'affiliated'
- □ *oleava* '(he/she) greased'
- □ *raleava* '(it) became thinner'

☛ **Check your answers with the Key.**

CD1—track 39

i. A dialogue to memorize.

Na praia

[without nasal vowels or diphthongs]

Cena: na praia
Personagens: Guto e Tê

Tê: Pô, Guto, que calor!
Guto: Pera aí, vou pegar a barraca.
T: Mas cadê a barraca?
G: Ficou no carro.
T: Ficou no carro? E cadê o carro?
G: Está ali mesmo. . . . Opa! Cadê o carro? Foi rebocado, ou foi roubado!
T: E agora? Voltar a pé?
G: A pé. É mole, gata. Só três ou quatro horas. Vai ser gostoso.
T: É, eu queria me queimar, mas isso já é exagero.

E agora? Voltar a pé?

Lesson 16

Nasal vowel [ɐ̃]

Portuguese has a distinction, not found in English, between oral and nasal vowels. This is not to say that there are no nasal vowels in English; for instance, the vowel in *hunt* is usually nasal in American pronunciation and is very close to Portuguese **a** in *canto* '(I) sing,' pronounced [ɐ̃]. But the nasal vowel in *hunt* is "felt" by English speakers to be identical to the **u** of *hut* followed by an **n**; this is not strictly true, as spectrographic analysis shows, but it is psychologically real, and that is the important thing as far as perceiving sounds of the language is concerned. We can say that English has oral and nasal vowels, but without a phonological opposition between them.

English does distinguish between oral and nasal consonants. Pronounce the pair *bee–me* several times. You will find that for [m] the air comes out through the nose, whereas for [b] no air comes out through the nose (in fact, during the pronunciation of the consonant, no air comes out at all). This effect is achieved by lowering, for the nasals, the velum (the fleshy part of the palate) so that air can escape through the nose. A nasal vowel is produced by the same mechanism; but the velum is only half-lowered so that air can escape *simultaneously* through nose and mouth.

Portuguese has five nasal vowels: [ɐ̃] (written **ã** or, before a nasal consonant, **a/â**), [õ] (written **õ** or, before a nasal consonant, **o/ô**), [ẽ, ĩ, ũ] (written **e/ê, i/í, u/ú**, respectively, before a nasal consonant). The difference between oral and nasal **a** is easy to perceive because nasal **a** is pronounced with the lower jaw much

49

higher (more closed) than it is for oral **a**; this accounts for a very clear difference in sound. With the other four nasal vowels the difference is more subtle, involving nasality alone. We correspondingly begin with nasal **a**.

The nasal vowel [ɐ̃] is written **ã, â** or just **a.** The latter spelling occurs when **a** is (1) before **nh**; (2) before **n** or **m** + another consonant; or (3) when stressed and before **n** or **m.**

CD1 — track 40

a. Listen.

[a] / [ɐ̃]

ajo [ˈaːʒu]	'(I) act'
anjo [ˈɐ̃ːʒu]	'angel'
laça [ˈlaːsə]	'(he/she) lassoes'
lança [ˈlɐ̃ːsə]	'spear'
mato [ˈmaːtu]	'thicket'
manto [ˈmɐ̃ːtu]	'mantle'
lá [ˈlaː]	'there'
lã [ˈlɐ̃ː]	'wool'
tato [ˈtaːtu]	'touch'
tanto [ˈtɐ̃ːtu]	'so much'
escovado [iskoˈvaːdu]	'brushed'
escovando [iskoˈvɐ̃ːdu]	'brushing'
caçado [kaˈsaːdu]	'hunted'
cansado [kɐ̃ˈsaːdu]	'tired'
laçou [laˈsoː]	'(he/she) lassoed'
lanço [laˈsoː]	'(he/she) threw'

STRESSED [ɐ̃] BEFORE A NASAL CONSONANT

fama [ˈfɐ̃ːmə]	'fame'
cano [ˈkɐ̃ːnu]	'pipe, tube'
câmera [ˈkɐ̃ːmerə]	'camera'
chame [ˈʃɐ̃ːmi]	'call [imperative]'
pano [ˈpɐ̃ːnu]	'fabric'

pânico ['pɐ̃ːniku]	'panic'
banana [ba'nɐ̃ːnə]	'banana'
ramo ['hɐ̃ːmu]	'branch'

WORD-FINAL [ɐ̃]

irmã [ih'mɐ̃ː]	'sister'
ímã ['iːmɐ̃]	'magnet'
maçã [ma'sɐ̃ː]	'apple'
órfã ['ɔːhfɐ̃]	'(female) orphan'

b. Listen again. Repeat aloud after each word.

c. Read each word aloud.

CD1 — track 41

d. Listen.

Chame a sua irmã.	'Call your sister.'
Diana parece um anjo.	'Diana looks like an angel.'
Júlio planta bananas e maçãs.	'Júlio grows bananas and apples.'
Diana era órfã.	'Diana was an orphan.'
Fernando começou a cantar.	'Fernando began to sing.'
Xande cansou logo.	'Xande got tired right away.'

e. Listen again. Repeat aloud after each sentence.

f. Read each sentence aloud.

CD1 — track 42

g. Listen, then check the word you have heard: the one with [a] or the one with [ɐ̃].

Diana parece um anjo

[a]

- [ ] *lá* 'there'
- [ ] *Sá* (surname)
- [ ] *vá* 'go'
- [ ] *maca* 'stretcher'
- [ ] *abas* 'brims'
- [ ] *mata* 'woods'
- [ ] *grade* 'grate'
- [ ] *caça* 'hunt'
- [ ] *machucado* 'injured'
- [ ] *catando* 'picking up'

[ã]

- [ ] *lã* 'wool'
- [ ] *sã* 'healthy [feminine]'
- [ ] *van* 'van'
- [ ] *manca* 'lame [feminine]'
- [ ] *ambas* 'both [feminine]'
- [ ] *manta* 'blanket'
- [ ] *grande* 'large'
- [ ] *cansa* '(he/she) tires'
- [ ] *machucando* 'hurting'
- [ ] *cantando* 'singing'

☞ **Check your answers with the Key.**

Lesson 17

Nasal vowels [ẽ, õ]

The vowels [ẽ] and [õ] (written **e** or **ê** and **o** or **ô,** respectively) are the nasalized counterparts of [e] and [o]; the vowels [ɛ] and [ɔ] never nasalize. The sound [ẽ] never occurs word-finally; there it is replaced by the diphthong [ẽj] (see Lesson 19).

CD1 — track 43

a. Listen.

[e] / [ẽ]

seda ['seːdə]	'silk'
senda ['sẽːdə]	'path'
vedado [ve'daːdu]	'forbidden'
vendado [vẽ'daːdu]	'blindfolded'
queixa ['keːʃə]	'complaint'
encha ['ẽːʃə]	'fill [imperative]'

STRESSED [ẽ] BEFORE A NASAL CONSONANT

ema ['ẽːmə]   'rhea'

problema [proˈblẽːmə]   'problem'
remo [ˈhẽːmu]   'paddle'
Breno [ˈbrẽːnu]   (man's name)
menos [ˈmẽːnus]   'less'
Marlene [mahˈlẽːni]   (woman's name)

sêmen [ˈsẽːmẽj]   'semen'
tênis [ˈtẽːnis]   'tennis'
pêndulo [ˈpẽːdulu]   'pendulum'

[o] / [õ]

tou [ˈtoː]   '(I) am'
tom [ˈtõː]   'key (music)'
sou [ˈsoː]   '(I) am'
som [ˈsõː]   'sound (noise)'

boba [ˈboːbə]   'stupid [feminine]'
bomba [ˈbõːbə]   'bomb'
coxa [ˈkoːʃə]   'thigh'
concha [ˈkõʃə]   'ladle'
otário [oˈtaːɾju]   'sucker'
Ontário [õˈtaːɾju]   'Ontario'

fosso [ˈfoːsu]   'ditch'
Afonso [aˈfõːsu]   (man's name)
louco [ˈloːku]   'crazy'
ronco [ˈhõku]   'snore'

WORD-FINAL [õ]

marrom [maˈhõː]   'brown'
batom [baˈtõː]   'lipstick'

STRESSED [õ] BEFORE A NASAL CONSONANT

zona [ˈzõːnə]   'zone'
como [ˈkõːmu]   'like, as'
soma [ˈsõːmə]   'sum'
sono [ˈsõːnu]   'sleep'

ônibus [ˈõːnibus]   'bus'
pônei [ˈpõːnej]   'pony'

b. Listen again. Repeat aloud after each word.

c. Read each word aloud.

CD1 — track 44

d. Listen.

Ela tá de batom branco.   'She has white lipstick on.'
O Breno está com sono.   'Breno is sleepy.'
Encha uma concha de sopa.   'Fill a ladle with soup.'

Encha uma concha de sopa

Afonso comprou pano marrom.   'Afonso bought brown cloth.'
A gente vende banana.   'We sell bananas.'
A Marlene trabalha cada vez menos.   'Marlene works less and less.'
Esse é o problema.   'That is the problem.'

e. Listen again. Repeat aloud after each sentence.

f. Read each sentence aloud.

CD1—track 45

g. Listen, then check the word you have heard: the one with [e] or the one with [ẽ].

[e]	[ẽ]
☐ *Leda* (woman's name)	☐ *lenda* 'legend'
☐ *violeta* 'violet'	☐ *violenta* 'violent [feminine]'
☐ *eixo* 'axle'	☐ *encho* '(I) fill'
☐ *cedo* 'early'	☐ *sendo* 'being'
☐ *fedeu* '(it) stank'	☐ *fendeu* '(it) split'

☞ Check your answers with the Key.

CD1—track 46

h. Listen, then check the word you have heard: the one with [o] or the one with [õ].

[o]	[õ]
☐ *sou* '(I) am'	☐ *som* 'sound (noise)'
☐ *dou* '(I) give'	☐ *dom* 'gift'
☐ *boba* 'silly [feminine]'	☐ *bomba* 'bomb'
☐ *coxa* 'thigh'	☐ *concha* 'ladle'
☐ *otário* 'sucker'	☐ *Ontário* 'Ontario'

☞ Check your answers with the Key.

Lesson 18

Nasal vowels [ĩ, ũ]

> The vowels [ĩ] and [ũ] are written **i, í** and **u, ú**, respectively, and always occur before **n, nh,** or **m.**
>
> I prefer to refer to the *letters* **n, nh, m** (rather than to the corresponding *sounds*) because **n** and **m** sometimes are not pronounced at all—and yet have the nasalizing effect.

CD1—track 47

a. Listen.

[i] / [ĩ]

lida [ˈliːdə]	'read [past participle, feminine]'
linda [ˈlĩːdə]	'beautiful [feminine]'
Aída [aˈiːdə]	(woman's name)
ainda [aˈĩːdə]	'still'
vi [ˈviː]	'(I) saw'
vim [ˈvĩː]	'(I) came'
si [ˈsiː]	'B (musical note)'
sim [ˈsĩː]	'yes'
vida [ˈviːdə]	'life'
vinda [ˈvĩːdə]	'coming'
kit [ˈkiːtʃi]	'kit'

vinte ['vĩːtʃi]	'twenty'
fita ['fiːtə]	'ribbon'
finta ['fĩːtə]	'feint'

[ĩ] BEFORE A NASAL CONSONANT + CONSONANT

xingando [ʃĩ'gʌdu]	'cursing'
empada [ĩ'paːdə]	(kind of small quiche)
imbecil [ĩbe'siːw]	'imbecile'
pinguço [pĩ'guːsu]	'drunkard'

STRESSED [ĩ] BEFORE A NASAL CONSONANT

fino ['fĩːnu]	'thin'
China ['ʃĩːnə]	'China'
menino [mĩ'nĩːnu]	'boy'
vime ['vĩːmi]	'wicker'
vindima [vĩ'dʒĩːmə]	'vintage'
mimo ['mĩːmu]	'caress'
química ['kĩːmikə]	'chemistry'
cínico ['sĩːniku]	'cynical'

[u] / [ũ]

o [u]	'the'
um [ũ]	'a [article]'
o gato [u'gaːtu]	'the cat'
um gato [ũ'gaːtu]	'a cat'
mudo ['muːdu]	'mute'
mundo ['mũːdu]	'world'
fuga ['fuːgə]	'flight'
funga ['fũːgə]	'(he/she) sniffs'
tatu [ta'tuː]	'armadillo'
atum [a'tũː]	'tuna'
tuba ['tuːbə]	'tuba'
tumba ['tũːbə]	'grave (tomb)'

[ũ] BEFORE A NASAL CONSONANT + CONSONANT

umbigo [ũ'biːgu]	'navel'
funcionário [fũsjo'naːɾju]	'employee'

suntuoso [sũtuˈoːzu]   'sumptuous'
Hungria [ũˈgɾiːjə]   'Hungary'
mungunzá [mũgũˈzaː]   'sweet grits'

STRESSED [ũ] BEFORE A NASAL CONSONANT

uma [ũːmə]   'one [feminine]'
puma [ˈpũːmə]   'cougar'
fume [ˈfũːmi]   '(he/she) smokes [subjunctive]'
húmus [ˈũːmus]   'humus'
alguma [awˈgũːmə]   'some [feminine]'
duna [ˈdũːnə]   'dune'
runa [ˈhũːnə]   'rune'
imune [iˈmũːni]   'immune'

b. Listen again. Repeat aloud after each word.

c. Read each word aloud.

CD1 — track 48

d. Listen.

Cida é linda.   'Cida is beautiful.'
Sim, toque um si.   'Yes, play a B.'
Recebi vinte kits da China.   'I received twenty kits from China.'

Rui é imune à gripe.   'Rui is immune to the flu.'
Um gato roubou o atum.   'A cat stole the tuna.'
O gato pegou alguma doença.   'The cat caught some kind of disease.'

Breno tocava tuba junto à tumba.   'Breno played the tuba by the grave.'

O mundo ficou mudo diante da tragédia.   'The world remained silent before the tragedy.'

e. Listen again. Repeat aloud after each sentence.

f. Read each sentence aloud.

CD1 — track 49

g. Listen, then check the word you have heard: the one with [i] or the one with [ĩ].

[i]	[ĩ]
☐ *vi* '(I) saw'	☐ *vim* '(I) came'
☐ *mi* 'E (musical note)'	☐ *mim* 'me'
☐ *ri* '(I) laughed'	☐ *rim* 'kidney'
☐ *vida* 'life'	☐ *vinda* 'coming'
☐ *fica* '(he/she) stays'	☐ *finca* '(he/she) drives in'
☐ *lipo* 'lipoaspiration surgery'	☐ *limpo* 'clean'

☞ **Check your answers with the Key.**

CD1 — track 50

h. Listen, then check the word you have heard: the one with [u] or the one with [ũ].

[u]	[ũ]
☐ *o* 'the'	☐ *um* 'a'
☐ *o gato* 'the cat'	☐ *um gato* 'a cat'
☐ *o peixe* 'the fish'	☐ *um peixe* 'a fish'
☐ *tuba* 'tuba'	☐ *tumba* 'grave'
☐ *mudo* 'mute'	☐ *mundo* 'world'
☐ *fuga* 'flight'	☐ *funga* '(he/she) sniffs'

☞ **Check your answers with the Key.**

CD1 — track 51

i. A dialogue to memorize:

O novo emprego

[nasal vs. oral vowels]

Cena: no escritório
Personagens: Tita e o chefe

CHEFE: Tita, essa é a sua mesa.

TITA: Já vi. Eu vim aqui hoje cedo.

C: Hoje cedo? Sendo assim, você já pode começar.

T: Claro, já posso começar. Assim o serviço rende mais.

C: Ô Tita, você vai precisar de tinta?

T: Tinta só mais tarde. Vou ficar lendo o texto, primeiro.

C: E depois?

T: Depois que tiver lido, aí vou imaginar uns desenhos. Vai ficar lindo, pode crer.

C: Assim espero. A antiga desenhista era uma bomba; era até meio boba.

T: Ela era boba, mas eu tenho experiência de vários anos.

Tita, essa é a sua mesa

Lesson 19

Nasal semivowel [j̃]

The sound [j̃] is the nasalized version of the semivowel [j] found in *baia* [ˈbaːjə] 'stall' and *lei* [ˈleːj] 'law.' Whenever [j̃] occurs, the preceding vowel is also nasalized, so a nasal diphthong results. This semivowel is written **nh** when between vowels: *banho* [ˈbɐ̃ːj̃u] 'bath,' *lenha* [ˈlẽːj̃ə] 'firewood.' Otherwise, it is mostly written **e,** and the preceding vowel bears a tilde: *mães* [ˈmɐ̃ːj̃s] 'mothers,' *põe* [ˈpõːj̃] '(he/she) puts.' In very rare cases it may be written **i**: *cãibra* [ˈkɐ̃ːj̃brə] 'cramp,' *Jaime* [ˈʒɐ̃ːj̃mi] (man's name), *muito* [ˈmũːj̃tu] 'very; much.' The most frequent sequence containing [j̃] is the diphtong [ẽj̃], written **-em** (or, in very few words, **-en**) word-finally: *bem* [ˈbẽːj̃] 'well,' *correm* [ˈkɔːhẽj̃] '(they) run.' A final **-ens** usually occurs in plural forms like *bens* [ˈbẽːj̃s] 'goods, assets.'

The pronunciation of **nh** (in spite of what some grammar books say) is *not* identical to that of Spanish **ñ** or French and Italian **gn,** although these may serve as a rough approximation. To pronounce Spanish **ñ** or French or Italian **gn** the tongue comes into contact with the palate, whereas for Portuguese **nh** the tongue only approaches the palate, so the result is the semivowel (or glide) [j̃], not a true consonant.

62

CD2 — track 1

a. Listen.

banho ['bɐ̃ːʒ̃u]	'bath'	
tenha ['tẽːʒ̃ə]	'(he/she) has [subjunctive]'	
sonha ['sõːʒ̃ə]	'(he/she) dreams'	
punho ['pũːʒ̃u]	'fist'	
vinho ['vĩːʒ̃u]	'wine'	

STRESSED [ẽj̃]

bem ['bẽːj̃]	'well, good'
alguém [awˈgẽːj̃]	'someone'
Belém [beˈlẽːj̃]	(city in Brazil)
gens ['ʒẽːj̃s]	'genes'
armazéns [ahmaˈzẽːj̃s]	'grocery stores'

UNSTRESSED [ẽj̃]

mandem ['mɐ̃ːdẽj̃]	'(they) order [subjunctive]'
vendem ['vẽːdẽj̃]	'(they) sell'
sobem ['sɔːbẽj̃]	'(they) go up'
hífen ['iːfẽj̃]	'hyphen'
nuvens ['nuːvẽj̃s]	'clouds'

mãe ['mɐ̃ːj̃]	'mother'
alemães [aleˈmɐ̃ːj̃s]	'Germans'
põe ['põːj̃]	'(he/she) puts'
põem ['põːj̃]	'(they) put' [same pronunciation as *põe*]
muito ['mũːj̃tu]	'much; very'

[ej] / [ẽj̃]

sem [sẽːj̃]	'without'
sei ['seːj]	'(I) know'
além [aˈlẽːj̃]	'beyond'
a lei [aˈleːj]	'the law'

bens ['bẽːj̃s]	'goods; assets'
seis ['seːjs]	'six'
tenha ['tẽːj̃ə]	'(he/she) has [subjunctive]'
teia ['teːjə]	'web'

[ij] / [ĩj̃]; [uj] / [ũj̃]

vinha ['vĩːj̃ə]	'(he/she) came'
via ['viːjə]	'(he/she) saw'
ruim ['hũːj̃]	'bad'
Rui ['huːj]	(man's name)

UNSTRESSED [ẽj̃] / [i]

mande ['mʌ̃ːdʒi]	'(he/she) order [subjunctive]'
mandem ['mʌ̃ːdẽj̃]	'(they) order [subjunctive]'
sobe ['sɔːbi]	'(he/she) goes up'
sobem ['sɔːbẽj̃]	'(they) go up'

[j̃] / [nj]

sonha ['sõːj̃ə]	'(he/she) dreams'
Sônia ['sõːnjə]	(woman's name)
ponho ['põːj̃u]	'(I) put'
Antônio [ʌ̃'tõːnju]	(man's name)

b. Listen again. Repeat aloud after each word.

c. Read each word aloud.

CD2 — track 2

d. Listen.

Antônio tomou banho em Belém.	'Antônio took a bath in Belém.'
César vinha, via e vencia.	'Caesar came, saw, and conquered.'
Esse carro sobe muito bem.	'This car goes uphill very well.'
Esses carros sobem muito bem.	'These cars go uphill very well.'

Eu sei comer sem guardanapo.	'I can eat without a napkin.'
As nuvens cobrem o céu.	'The clouds cover the sky.'
O peixe come folhas, e os gatos comem peixe.	'The fish eats leaves, and the cats eat fish.'

Os gatos comem peixe

e. **Listen again. Repeat aloud after each sentence.**

f. **Read each sentence aloud.**

CD2 — track 3

g. **Listen, then check the word you have heard: the one with [aj] or the one with [ãj̃].**

[aj]

☐ *cais* 'wharf'

[ãj̃]

☐ *cães* 'dogs'

☐ *maia* 'Maya (member of an Indian nation)'

☐ *manha* 'tantrum'

☐ *pais* 'parents'

☐ *pães* 'loaves'

☐ *mais* 'more'

☐ *mães* 'mothers'

☐ *baia* 'stall'

☐ *banha* 'lard'

☞ **Check your answers with the Key.**

CD2 — track 4

h. Listen, then check the word you have heard: the one with [ej] or the one with [ẽ j̃]).

[ej]

☐ *sei* '(I) know'

☐ *Nei* (man's name)

☐ *a lei* 'the law'

☐ *leia* 'read'

☐ *ceia* 'supper'

☐ *teia* 'web'

[ẽ j̃]

☐ *sem* 'without'

☐ *nem* 'not even'

☐ *além* 'beyond'

☐ *lenha* 'firewood'

☐ *senha* 'password'

☐ *tenha* '(I) have [subjunctive]'

☞ **Check your answers with the Key.**

Lesson 20

Nasal diphthong [Ãw̃]

🖉 The diphthong [Ãw̃] (written **ão** when stressed, **am** and rarely **ão** when unstressed) is very frequent in Portuguese, particularly at the ends of words. It is composed of the sound [Ã], studied in Lesson 16, plus a semivowel identical to [w] *but nasalized;* that is, the diphthong is nasalized throughout. The best way to acquire this pronunciation is to listen carefully to the recording and try to imitate it.

CD2 — track 5

---

a. Listen.

STRESSED [Ãw̃]

não ['nÃ:w̃]	'no'[1]
chão ['ʃÃ:w̃]	'floor'
portão [poh'tÃ:w̃]	'gate'
estão [is'tÃ:w̃]	'(they) are'
mãos ['mÃ:w̃s]	'hands'
irmãos [ih'mÃ:w̃s]	'brothers'

[1] The word *não* is frequently pronounced [nũ] when preceding a verb: *não sei* [nũ'sej] '(I) don't know.'

UNSTRESSED [Ãw̃]

falam ['faːlÃw̃]	'(they) speak'
correram [koˈheːɾÃw̃]	'(they) ran'
faziam [faˈziːjÃw̃]	'(they) made'
falavam [faˈlaːvÃw̃]	'(they) spoke'
órfão ['ɔːhfÃw̃]	'orphan'

[Ãw̃] / [aw]

pão ['pÃːw̃]	'bread'
pau ['paːw]	'stick'
mão ['mÃːw̃]	'hand'
mal ['maːw]	'poorly; ill'
são ['sÃːw̃]	'healthy'
sal ['saːw]	'salt'

[Ãw̃] / [Ã]

são ['sÃːw̃]	'healthy'
sã ['sÃː]	'healthy [feminine]'
irmão [ihˈmÃːw̃]	'brother'
irmã [ihˈmÃː]	'sister'
órfão ['ɔːhfÃw̃]	'orphan'
órfã ['ɔːhfÃ]	'orphan [feminine]'

[Ãw̃] / [õ]

são ['sÃːw̃]	'healthy'
som ['sõː]	'sound (noise)'
tão ['tÃːw̃]	'so much'
tom ['tõː]	'key (music)'
carrão [kaˈhÃːw̃]	'big car'
marrom [maˈhõː]	'brown'

b. Listen again. Repeat aloud after each word.

c. Read each word aloud.

CD2 — track 6

d. Listen.

Minhas mãos doíam demais.	'My hands hurt a lot.'
Não brinque no portão.	'Don't play at the gate.'
Os dois irmãos são órfãos.	'The two brothers are orphans.'
Elas faziam pão de sal e vendiam.	'They made and sold French bread.'
Os pães caíram no chão.	'The loaves fell on the floor.'
Seu som é tão bom quanto o de João.	'Your tone is as good as João's.'

e. Listen again. Repeat aloud after each sentence.

f. Read each sentence aloud.

CD2 — track 7

g. Listen, then check the word you have heard: the one with [aw] or the one with [ãw̃].

[aw]

☐ *pau* 'stick'
☐ *cal* 'lime'
☐ *mal* 'evil'
☐ *sinal* 'sign'
☐ *capital* 'capital'

[ãw̃]

☐ *pão* 'loaf'
☐ *cão* 'dog'
☐ *mão* 'hand'
☐ *senão* 'or else'
☐ *capitão* 'captain'

☛ **Check your answers with the Key.**

CD2 — track 8

h. A dialogue to memorize:

Consertos domésticos

[diphthong ão]

Cena: em casa
Personagens: Carla e João

João *[entrando em casa, irritado]:* Agora é o portão! Enguiçou! Tive que deixar o carro na rua, nesse solão.

Carla: João, João, meu querido! Por que essa irritação?

J: O portão da garagem! Não abriu de jeito nenhum. O controle não funciona, e eu não vou abrir na mão.

C: Devo chamar o eletricista?

J: Não! Já gastei demais a semana passada consertando o chão da cozinha. E custou um dinheirão. O portão só no mês que vem.

C: Quem sabe eu consigo abrir o portão?

Já consertei o controle

J: Você? Se eu que sou engenheiro não consegui, como é que você vai conseguir?

C: Ora, João! Você é engenheiro civil, não sabe nada de portão eletrônico. Olha, me dá aqui o controle.

[C abre o controle]

C: Já consertei o controle, senhor engenheiro.

J: Você mudou de profissão?

C: Não. Só coloquei uma pilha nova.

Lesson 21

Triphthongs and vocalic sequences

🎧 At this point, the student will have learned all the sounds of the Portuguese language. What remain are *sequences* of sounds—namely, triphthongs, vocalic sequences, and proparoxytone words—that are likely to present difficulties, plus some other refinements, including further models of intonational contours. These points are covered in Lessons 21–32.

Triphthongs

🎧 Triphthongs are sequences of a semivowel plus a vowel plus another semivowel. English has triphthongs in the exclamation *wow!* and in the word *way.* Triphthongs, like diphthongs, always belong to one and the same syllable.

We may have a triphthong whenever the letters **i** or **u,** which are often pronounced as semivowels, precede a diphthong. Six triphthongs actually occur in Portuguese: [waj], written **uai;** [wej], written **üei;** [waw], written **ual;** [wɐ̃w̃], written **uão** or **uam;** [wẽj̃], written **üem;** and [wõj̃], written **uõe.**

Triphthongs are not very frequent in the language, and they almost always occur after **q** or **g;** their pronunciation should not be particularly difficult for students who have learned to pronounce the diphthongs.

CD2 — track 9

a. Listen.

quais [ˈkwaːjs]	'which [plural]'
Paraguai [paɾaˈgwaːj]	'Paraguay'
uruguaio [uɾuˈgwaːju]	'Uruguayan'
agüei [aˈgweːj]	'(I) watered'
qual [ˈkwaːw]	'which'
igualmente [igwawˈmẽːtʃi]	'equally'
saguão [saˈgwʌ̃ːw̃]	'hall'
aguam [ˈaːgwʌ̃w̃]	'(they) water'
ágüem [ˈaːgwẽj̃]	'(they) water [subjunctive]'
saguões [saˈgwõːj̃s]	'lobbies'

b. Listen again. Repeat aloud after each word.

c. Read each word aloud.

Vocalic Sequences

> ✒ Many English speakers have trouble pronouncing Portuguese words with vocalic sequences—that is, sequences of contiguous vowels or semivowels—as found in words like *maioria* 'majority' and *reunião* 'meeting.' This difficulty seems to be more serious when the sequences are unstressed, and it is common enough to deserve specific consideration.

CD2 — track 10

d. Listen.

maior [maˈjɔːh]	'bigger'
oriental [oɾiẽˈtaːw]	'eastern'
realizou [healiˈzoː]	'(he/she) achieved'
atualmente [atuawˈmẽːtʃi]	'nowadays'
veiculava [veikuˈlaːvə]	'(he/she) conveyed'

maioria [majo'riːjə]	'majority'
reunião [heuni'ʎ̃ːw]	'meeting'
baioneta [bajo'neːtə]	'bayonet'
taoísmo [tao'iːzmu]	'Daoism'
sexualidade [seksuali'daːdʒi]	'sexuality'
extraordinário [istɾaohdʒi'naːɾju]	'extraordinary'
Piauí [pia'wiː]	(name of a Brazilian state)
continuidade [kõtʃinui'daːdʒi]	'continuity'
influência [ĩflu'ẽːsjə]	'influence'
piauiense [piawi'ẽːsi]	'born in Piauí'

e. Listen again. Repeat aloud after each word.

f. Read each word aloud.

Os veículos atuais são extraordinários

CD2 — track 11

g. Listen.

Quais eram as maiores influências?	'Which were the main influences?'
A reunião é no saguão.	'The meeting is in the lobby.'
O Uruguai também se chama "Banda Oriental."	'Uruguay is also called the Eastern Shore.'
Os veículos atuais são extraordinários.	'The latest vehicles are extraordinary.'
Qual é a capital do Piauí?	'Which is the capital of Piauí?'

h. Listen again. Repeat aloud after each sentence.

i. Read each sentence aloud.

Lesson 22

Inserted [i]

🖋 Although an inserted [i] does not present any difficulty in itself—being pronounced like any unstressed **i**—it occurs in written words that in English are pronounced without an [i]. This is a two-way problem: English speakers fail to insert an [i] in, say, *optar* 'to opt,' which in Portuguese sounds like [opiˈtaːh], not [opˈtaːh]; and Portuguese speakers insist on starting a word like *stay* with an [i], pronouncing it [iˈstej] instead of [ˈstej]. The rules governing **i**-insertion are stated in full in *Modern Portuguese,* section 3.5.

The exercises in this lesson will help the student develop a more natural, Brazilian-sounding pronunciation of certain words. Many of these, as seen below, are loanwords with non-Portuguese features like final **-t** and initial **sp-**.

CD2 — track 12

a. Listen.

optei [opiˈteːj]	(I) chose'
advogado [adʒivoˈgaːdu]	'lawyer'
Sidney [ˈsiːdʒinej]	(man's name)
magno [ˈmaːginu]	'great'
atmosfera [atʃimɔsˈfɛːrə]	'atmosphere'
admirava [adʒimiˈraːvə]	'(he/she) admired'
pitbull [pitʃiˈbuːw]	'pit bull'

76

stress [isˈtɾɛːs]; [also written *estresse*]	'(psychological) stress'
stalinismo [istaliˈniːzmu]	'Stalinism'
spray [isˈpɾeːj]	'aerosol'
spread [isˈpɾɛːdʒi]	'spread (banking)'
status [isˈtaːtus]	'status'
staccato [istaˈkaːtu]	'staccato'
Skank [isˈkʌ̃ːki]	(name of a rock band)
set [ˈsɛːtʃi]	'set (in volleyball)'
deck [ˈdɛːki]	'console'
rap [ˈhɛːpi]	'rap (music)'
rock [ˈhɔːki]	'rock 'n' roll'
top [ˈtɔːpi]	'top, leading'
USP [ˈuːspi]	'USP (University of São Paulo)'

b. Listen again. Repeat aloud after each word.

c. Read each word aloud.

> CD2 — track 13

d. Listen.

Ando no maior stress.	'(I) am stressed out.'
Sidney tinha um pitbull.	'Sidney had a pit bull.'
O Skank só toca rock.	'The Skank plays only rock 'n' roll.'
Optei pelo melhor advogado.	'(I) chose the best lawyer.'
Tocar rap não dá status.	'Playing rap doesn't give (one) status.'
Admiro a atmosfera agradável da USP.	'(I) admire the pleasant environment at USP.'

e. Listen again. Repeat aloud after each sentence.

f. Read each sentence aloud.

CD2 — track 14

g. A dialogue to memorize:

Jogo decisivo

[inserted [i]; English loanwords]

Cena: no vestiário
Personagens: Fred e o treinador (Sidney)

SIDNEY: Olha, Fred, outra dessa e eu corto o seu nome da equipe! Perder no último set!
FRED: Mas, seu Sidney, isso pode acontecer com qualquer um.
S: O que foi que aconteceu?

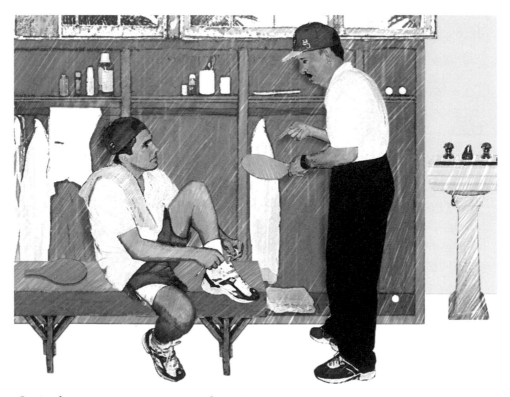

Outra dessa e eu corto o seu nome da equipe

F: Eu tentei aquela jogada que eu inventei lá nos States. Deu certo várias vezes, já virou standard.

S: Mas dessa vez a bola foi pro chão, né?

F: No último set eu já tava cansado. E eu tava no maior stress. Tive uma conversa com o advogado de manhã.

S: Você devia optar: ou o divórcio, ou o pingue-pongue.

F: Agora eu já tou mais calmo. Na próxima partida eu vou voltar ao meu ritmo, vou arrasar.

S: Acho bom, Fred. Senão você não tem chance de ir pra Olimpíada.

F: Meu negócio com a Margaret vai resolver essa semana. Aí a atmosfera vai ficar melhor.

S: Mas lembra bem: a bola é na mesa, não no chão. Isso aqui é pingue-pongue, e não golfe.

F: Deixa comigo, seu Sidney. O maior interessado sou eu: é o meu status que tá em jogo.

Lesson 23

Proparoxytones

🎵 Proparoxytones are words stressed on the second-to-last syllable: *último* ['uːwtʃi- mu] 'last,' *lingüística* [lĩ'gwiːstʃikə] 'linguistics.' All proparoxytones bear an accent on the stressed vowel. The examples in this lesson will help the student acquire their peculiar rhythm, consisting of a long stressed syllable followed by two very short ones; the latter, when before a pause, often become unvoiced.

CD2 — track 15

a. Listen.

xícara ['ʃiːkərə]	'cup'
máquina ['maːkinə]	'machine'
tímida ['tʃiːmidə]	'shy [feminine]'
pálida ['paːlidə]	'pale [feminine]'
lâmpada ['lɐ̃ːpədə]	'light bulb'
Drácula ['draːkulə]	'Dracula (name)'
música ['muːzikə]	'music'
química ['kĩːmikə]	'chemistry'
espátula [is'paːtulə]	'spatula'
ridícula [hi'dʒiːkulə]	'ridiculous [feminine]'

80

México ['mɛːʃiku]	'Mexico'
século ['sɛːkulu]	'century'
médico ['mɛːdʒiku]	'physician'
máximo ['maːsimu]	'maximum'
ótimo ['ɔːtʃimu]	'excellent'
místico ['miːstʃiku]	'mystic'
lingüístico [lĩ'gwiːstʃiku]	'linguistic'
asmático [az'maːtʃiku]	'asthmatic'
estávamos [is'taːvəmus]	'(we) were'
fazíamos [fa'ziːjəmus]	'(we) made'

PROPAROXYTONES / PAROXYTONES (MINIMAL PAIRS)

médica ['mɛːdʒikə]	'physician'
medica [me'dʒiːkə]	'(he/she) medicates'
válido ['vaːlidu]	'valid'
valido [vali:du]	'protégé'
tônico ['tõːniku]	'tonic'
Tonico [tu'niːku]	(man's nickname)
vínculo ['vĩːkulu]	'bond'
vinculo [vĩ'kuːlu]	'(I) bind'
estímulo [is'tʃiːmulu]	'stimulus'
estimulo [istʃi'muːlu]	'(I) stimulate'

🖎 One effect of **i**-insertion (*Modern Portuguese*, 3.5; and see Lesson 22) is that some words which in their written form look like paroxytones (with a stress on the penultimate syllable) are in fact proparoxytones (with a stress on the third syllable from the end). For instance, *apto* 'able' is pronounced ['aːpitu]; the pronunciation ['aːptu] occurs only in very fast speech. Examples are:

ritmo ['hiːtʃimu]	'rhythm'
acne ['aːkini]	'acne'
apto ['aːpitu]	'able'
Edna ['ɛːdʒinə]	(woman's name)

Another effect of **i**-insertion is that some words are stressed on the *fourth* syllable from the end (although their written form suggests that they are proparoxytones). For instance:

> | | |
> |---|---|
> | *técnica* ['tɛːkinikə] | 'technique' |
> | *étnico* ['ɛːtʃiniku] | 'ethnic' |
> | *rítmico* ['hiːtʃimiku] | 'rhythmic' |

b. Listen again. Repeat aloud after each word.

c. Read each word aloud.

CD2 — track 16

d. Listen.

Edna estuda química.	'Edna studies chemistry.'
A música do México é ótima.	'Mexican music is excellent.'
Drácula apagou a lâmpada.	'Dracula turned off the light.'
Esse é um problema lingüístico.	'This is a linguistic problem.'
Nós sempre tomávamos uma xícara de chá.	'We always drank a cup of tea.'
Não entendo essa técnica.	'(I) don't understand that technique.'
Me interesso por estudos étnicos.	'(I)'m interested in ethnic studies.'

e. Listen again. Repeat aloud after each sentence.

f. Read each sentence aloud.

CD2 — track 17

g. Listen, then check the word you have heard: the word with a paroxytone or the one with a proparoxytone.

PAROXYTONES	PROPAROXYTONES
☐ *medica* '(he/she) medicates'	☐ *médica* 'physician'
☐ *Tonico* 'man's nickname'	☐ *tônico* 'tonic'
☐ *vomito* '(I) vomit'	☐ *vômito* 'vomit'

Edna estuda química

- □ *continuo* '(I) continue'
- □ *magoa* '(he/she) hurts'
- □ *florida* 'in flower [feminine]'
- □ *desanimo* '(I) discourage'

- □ *contínuo* 'continuous'
- □ *mágoa* 'sorrow'
- □ *Flórida* 'Florida'
- □ *desânimo* 'dejection'

⌐ **Check your answers with the Key.**

Lesson 24

Oxytones

🎵 Oxytones are words stressed on the last syllable: *armazém* [ahma'zẽːj] 'grocery store,' *estação* [ista'sᴧ̃ːw] 'season.' These words, especially when long, may be difficult to pronounce correctly because of their peculiar rhythm, which is unlike anything in English. English speakers tend to stress the first syllable, often rendering the word unrecognizable.

CD2 — track 18

a. Listen.

café [ka'fɛː]	'coffee'
avô [a'voː]	'grandfather'
está [is'taː]	'(he/she) is'
aqui [a'kiː]	'here'
tatu [ta'tuː]	'armadillo'
chaminé [ʃami'nɛː]	'chimney'
diretor [dʒiɾe'toːh]	'director'
algodão [awgu'dᴧ̃ːw]	'cotton'
semanal [sema'naːw]	'weekly'
esperava [ispe'raːvə]	'(he/she) waited'

acarajé [akaɾaˈʒɛː]   'fried bean cake'
agricultor [agɾikuwˈtoːh]   'farmer'
operação [opeɾaˈsʎ̃ːw]   'operation'
mandacaru [mʎ̃dakaˈɾuː]   (type of cactus)

b. Listen again. Repeat aloud after each word.

c. Read each word aloud.

CD2 — track 19

d. Listen.

ANALOGOUS PAIRS

farei [faˈɾeːj]   '(I) will make'
fáceis [ˈfaːsejs]   'easy [pl]'
paletó [paliˈtɔː]   'coat'
palito [paˈliːtu]   'toothpick'
maçã [maˈsʎ̃ː]   'apple'
massa [ˈmaːsə]   'pasta'
portão [pohˈtʎ̃ːw]   'gate'
porta [ˈpɔːhtə]   'door'

e. Listen again. Repeat aloud after each word.

f. Read each word aloud.

CD2 — track 20

g. Listen.

Vovô está aqui.   'Grandpa is here.'
Eu pedi mais café.   'I asked for more coffee.'
O diretor quer vender algodão. 'The director wants to sell cotton.'
Esta maçã está verde.   'This apple is green.'
Nosso jantar é semanal.   'Our dinner is once a week.'

Vovô está aqui

h. Listen again. Repeat aloud after each sentence.

i. Read each sentence aloud.

CD2 — track 21

j. Listen, then check the word you have heard: paroxytone or oxytone.

PAROXYTONES

☐ *tato* 'touch'
☐ *abre* '(he/she) opens'
☐ *tio* 'uncle'
☐ *pia* 'sink'

OXYTONES

☐ *tatu* 'armadillo'
☐ *abri* '(I) opened'
☐ *teú* (kind of lizard)
☐ *piá* 'little boy'

☐ *cantam* '(they) sing' ☐ *cantão* 'canton'
☐ *porem* '(they) put' ☐ *porém* 'however'

☞ **Check your answers with the Key.**

Lesson 25

Joining words: final **m, l,** and **r**

🔊 English speakers tend to pronounce final **m** and **l** as consonants, saying, for example, [ˈbɔm] and [ˈmɛɫ] for *bom* and *mel,* which should be pronounced [ˈbõ] and [ˈmɛw], respectively (see *Modern Portuguese,* 2.2). This tendency is especially strong when a vowel follows, so particular care must be taken to pronounce, say, *com Ana* 'with Ana' as [kõˈʌ̃nə], without any consonant before the **a** of *Ana.*

As for a final **r,** it is pronounced like [h] before a pause or a consonant, but like [ɾ] before a vowel in a following word (see Lesson 14; a final **r** is usually silent when in a verb form; see *Modern Portuguese,* 2.2).

CD2 — track 22

a. Listen.

massa sem ovos [ˈmaːsə sẽj ˈɔːvus]	'pasta without eggs'
massa com ovos [ˈmaːsə kõ ˈɔːvus]	'pasta with eggs'
eles moram aqui [ˈeːlis ˈmɔːɾʌ̃w̃ aˈkiː]	'they live here'
Joaquim Almeida [ʒuaˈkĩːj̃ awˈmeːjdə]	(man's full name)
um amigo [ũ aˈmiːgu]	'a friend'

b. Listen again. Repeat aloud after each phrase.

c. Read each phrase aloud.

CD2 — track 23

d. Listen.

mel azedo [ˈmɛːw aˈzeːdu]	'sour honey'	
curral aberto [kuˈhaːw aˈbɛːhtu]	'open corral'	
azul escuro [aˈzuːw isˈkuːru]	'dark blue'	
mil homens [ˈmiːw ˈõmẽĵs]	'a thousand men'	
móvel antigo [ˈmɔːvew ʎˈtʃiːgu]	'antique chest of drawers'	

e. Listen again. Repeat aloud after each phrase.

f. Read each phrase aloud.

CD2 — track 24

g. Listen.

cor [koːh]	'color'
cor branca [koːh ˈbrʎːkə]	'white color'
cor azul [ˈkoːɾ aˈzuːw]	'blue color'
mulher [muʎɛːh]	'woman'
mulher pobre [muˈʎɛːh ˈpɔːbɾi]	'poor woman'
mulher alta [muˈʎɛːɾ ˈaːwtə]	'tall woman'
mar [maːh]	'sea'
Mar do Norte [ˈmaːh du ˈnɔːhtʃi]	'North Sea'
Mar Egeu [ˈmaːɾ eˈʒeːw]	'Aegean Sea'
açúcar [aˈsuːkəh]	'sugar'
açúcar mascavo [aˈsuːkəh masˈkaːvu]	'brown sugar'
açúcar ótimo [aˈsuːkəɾ ˈɔːtʃimu]	'excellent sugar'

h. Listen again. Repeat aloud after each phrase.

i. Read each phrase aloud.

CD2 — track 25

j. Listen.

Sem água o motor esquenta.	'Without water the engine heats up.'
O motor do carro esquentou.	'The car's engine has heated up.'
A cor amarela é mais feia que a cor verde.	'The yellow color is uglier than the green color.'
Joaquim Almeida deixou o curral aberto.	'Joaquim Almeida left the corral open.'

k. Listen again. Repeat aloud after each sentence.

l. Read each sentence aloud.

Deixa que eu bato, Lucinha

CD2 — track 26

m. A dialogue to memorize:

Massa com ovos

[final *m*, *l*, and *r*]

Cena: na cozinha
Personagens: Mamãe e Lucinha

LUCINHA: Mamãe, como se faz massa com ovos?
MAMÃE: Massa com ovos?? Ora, igual a massa sem ovos; só que com ovos.
L: A gente pode pôr sal à vontade?
M: Claro que não, Lucinha. Só uma colher assim pelo meio.
L: E os ovos? Vai jogando e batendo?
M: Vai batendo até ficar uma cor amarela.
L *[batendo]:* Pô, mãe, tá ficando uma cor horrível.
M: Batendo devagar assim a massa vai ficar toda encaroçada. Tem que bater com força.
L: Vem aqui, mamãe, será que já tá bom assim?
M: Deixa que eu bato, Lucinha. Eta mulher incompetente!
L: Um dia eu aprendo, mãe.

Lesson 26

Joining words: vowel reduction

Certain vowel reductions occur in rapid, fluent speech.

When a word ends in an unstressed vowel and the following word also begins with an unstressed vowel, the first of these vowels is reduced: if the first vowel is [i] and the second one is not [i], the first vowel becomes a semivowel [j]; in all other cases the first vowel is dropped. If one or both of the vowels are stressed, they are both fully pronounced, and reduction does not take place.

This kind of reduction is not usual in Italian and is less frequent in Spanish than in Portuguese, so students who already know those languages should pay particular attention to vowel reduction, which is one of the features that give Portuguese speech its peculiar rhythm.

In slower speech, reduction occurs only when the two vowels in contact are identical, as in *casa aberta* [ˈkaːzaˈbɛːhtə] 'open house.'

CD2 — track 27

a. Listen.

bule [ˈbuːli]		'coffeepot'
bule horrível [ˈbuːljoˈhiːvew]		'awful coffeepot'
pele [ˈpɛːli]		'skin'
pele amarela [ˈpɛːljamaˈrɛːlə]		'yellow skin'

sobe [ˈsɔːbi]   '(he/she) goes up'
sobe a rampa [ˈsɔːbjəˈhɐ̃pə]   '(he/she) goes up the ramp'

b. Listen again. Repeat aloud after each word or phrase.

c. Read each word or phrase aloud.

CD2 — track 28

d. Listen.

Ela sobe o morro.   'She goes up the hill.'
Ele é sempre amável.   'He is always kind.'
Cale a boca.   'Shut up.'

Ele é sempre amável

e. Listen again. Repeat aloud after each sentence.

f. Read each sentence aloud.

CD2 — track 29

g. Listen.

casa [ˈkaːzə]	'house'
casa aberta [ˈkaːzaˈbɛːhtə]	'open house'
casa enorme [ˈkaːziˈnɔːhmi]	'huge house'
casa ocupada [ˈkaːzokuˈpaːdə]	'occupied house'
carro [ˈkaːhu]	'car'
carro elétrico [ˈkaːhɛˈlɛːtɾiku]	'electric car'
carro amassado [ˈkaːhamaˈsaːdu]	'car wrecked in a crash'
enrugada [ĩhuˈgaːdə]	'wrinkled'
pele enrugada [ˈpɛːlĩhuˈgaːdə]	'wrinkled skin'
emprestado [ĩpresˈtaːdu]	'borrowed'
bule emprestado [ˈbuːlĩpresˈtaːdu]	'borrowed coffeepot'

h. Listen again. Repeat aloud after each word or phrase.

i. Read each word or phrase aloud.

CD2 — track 30

j. Listen.

Meu pai é um cara ocupado.	'My father is a busy guy.'
Ela fala inglês.	'She speaks English.'
Esse dentista atende em casa.	'This dentist works at home.'

k. Read each sentence aloud.

Lesson 27

Stress patterns in cognates

Some words are very similar in Portuguese and English as far as their written form is concerned, but differ in pronunciation, especially in stress placement. Practicing their pronunciation will help block the tendency of the student to pronounce them in the English fashion and will help develop the habit of placing stress on the correct syllable.

The problem is particularly acute when the words involved are long (say, more than four syllables). For English speakers, the difficulty in pronouncing longer Portuguese words comes largely from a difference in rhythm. Compare, for instance, English *agriculture* and Portuguese *agricultura:* the English word is pronounced with a clear stress on the first and third syllables, whereas the Portuguese word is stressed on the second and fourth syllables (I am not distinguishing primary and secondary stress here). Moreover, unstressed (pre-stress) syllables are normally much shorter in English than in Portuguese—that is, Portuguese words have a more homogeneous rhythm, without too much difference in duration between syllables, whereas English words show a wider difference in duration between syllables. Long Portuguese words are correspondingly more difficult for English speakers to pronounce, in particular when they are similar to their English counterparts. The tendency is to pronounce Portuguese *agricultura* with the same rhythm as English *agriculture,* which makes for a heavily marked foreign accent.

The rules for placing primary and secondary stresses in Portuguese words are given in full in *Modern Portuguese*, 3.1. Here I give a systematic presentation of several stress patterns in words of four and more syllables. The student should listen carefully to the examples and attempt to reproduce the words with the correct distribution of long and short, stressed and unstressed syllables.

CD2 — track 31

a. Listen.

sincronização	[sĩkɾoniza'sɐ̃ːw]	'synchronization'
recondicionado	[hekõdʒisjo'naːdu]	'reconditioned'
desembaraçado	[dʒizĩbaɾa'saːdu]	'uninhibited'
televisionado	[televizjo'naːdu]	'televised'
tecnologia	[tɛkinolo'ʒiːjə]	'technology'

comunicação	[komunika'sɐ̃ːw]	'communication'
incondicional	[ĩkõdʒisjo'naːw]	'unconditional'
desestimulado	[dʒizistʃimu'laːdu]	'discouraged'
interrogação	[ĩtehoga'sɐ̃ːw]	'interrogation'

agricultura	[agɾikuw'tuːɾə]	'agriculture'
pacificando	[pasifi'kɐ̃ːdu]	'pacifying'
repetição	[hepetʃi'sɐ̃ːw]	'repetition'
carpintaria	[kahpĩta'ɾiːjə]	'carpentry'
temperatura	[tẽpeɾa'tuːɾə]	'temperature'
laboratório	[laboɾa'tɔːɾju]	'laboratory'

b. Listen again. Repeat aloud after each word.

c. Read each word aloud.

CD2 — track 32

d. Listen.

acidente	[asi'dẽːtʃi]	'accident'
diferente	[dʒife'ɾẽːtʃi]	'different'

elefante [ele'fʌ̃ːtʃi]	'elephant'
importante [ĩpoh'tʌ̃ːtʃi]	'important'
restaurante [hestaw'rʌ̃ːtʃi]	'restaurant'
agência [a'ʒẽːsjə]	'agency'
emergência [emeh'ʒẽːsjə]	'emergency'
freqüência [fre'kwẽːsjə]	'frequency'
infância [ĩ'fʌ̃ːsjə]	'childhood'
calendário [kalẽ'daːrju]	'calendar'
dicionário [dʒisjo'naːrju]	'dictionary'
hemisfério [emis'fɛːrju]	'hemisphere'
secretária [sekre'taːrjə]	'secretary'
bateria [bate'riːjə]	'battery'
cafeteria [kafete'riːjə]	'cafeteria'
categoria [katego'riːjə]	'category'
geografia [ʒeogra'fiːjə]	'geography'
animal [ani'maːw]	'animal'
papel [pa'pɛːw]	'paper'
delicioso [delisi'oːzu]	'delicious'
famoso [fa'moːzu]	'famous'
literatura [litera'tuːrə]	'literature'
aspirina [aspi'rĩːnə]	'aspirin'
hambúrguer [ʌ̃'buːhgeh]	'hamburger'
carpete [kah'pɛːtʃi]	'carpet'
chocolate [ʃoko'laːtʃi]	'chocolate'
momento [mo'mẽːtu]	'moment'
Paris [pa'riːs]	'Paris'
serviço [sih'viːsu]	'service'
sucesso [su'sɛːsu]	'success'
teatro [tʃi'aːtru]	'theater'
veículo [ve'iːkulu]	'vehicle'
vinagre [vi'naːgri]	'vinegar'
Europa [ew'rɔːpə]	'Europe'

e. Listen again. Repeat aloud after each word.

f. Read each word aloud.

CD2 — track 33

g. Listen.

Me dá uma aspirina e um hambúrguer.	'Give me an aspirin and a hamburger.'
Elza é uma secretária de sucesso.	'Elza is a successful secretary.'
Paris tem o melhor chocolate da Europa.	'Paris has the best chocolate in Europe.'
Isso é uma emergência: tem um elefante no restaurante.	'This is an emergency: there is an elephant in the restaurant.'

h) Listen again. Repeat aloud after each sentence.

i) Read each sentence aloud.

CD2 — track 34

g. A dialogue to memorize:

O acidente

[stress in cognates]

Cena: na rua
Personagens: policial e testemunha

POLICIAL: A senhora viu o acidente?
TESTEMUNHA: Vi, sim senhor. Eu ia entrando na catedral quando ouvi um barulhão de freio. Naquele momento o carro pegou o rapaz.
P: O veículo vinha em alta velocidade?
T: Não, seu guarda. Acho que o turista não prestou atenção no trânsito e foi pego de

Olha ali, no chão!

surpresa. Eu corri pro telefone, liguei pro hospital e esperei até que a ambulância chegou.

P: Turista? A senhora acha que ele é turista?

T: É, eu passei primeiro na farmácia pra comprar uma aspirina, e ele estava lá. Ninguém entendia o que ele queria. Até que ele apontou pra uma barra de chocolate e disse: "Quanto é?"

P: Será que ele é americano?

T: Parecia mais japonês. Espero que não esteja muito machucado.

P: Acho que só fraturou o braço. Podia ter sido muito pior.

T: Olha ali, no chão!

P: Quê que é?

T: É a barra de chocolate! Ele não teve nem tempo de comer.

Lesson 28

Intonation: declarative sentences vs. yes-no questions

Intonation cannot be learned by reading about it. Spoken models are indispensable, as is long practice. Lessons 25–28 present a few major intonational contours, along with some comments about their English counterparts.

As in English, Portuguese declarative sentences are marked by a falling final intonational contour. Yes-no questions (defined in *Modern Portuguese*, 31.1.1), on the other hand, have a final rising contour, and this is the main feature distinguishing them from declarative sentences. Subject-verb inversion, which is the feature distinguishing these two structures in English, is absent in Portuguese in most cases, so intonation is the only phonetic mark of yes-no questions, and the symbol '?' its only graphic mark.

CD2 — track 35

a. Listen.

Esse bolo foi feito com fubá.	'This cake was made with cornmeal.'
Esse bolo foi feito com fubá?	'Was this cake made with cornmeal?'
Seu pai já desistiu de se candidatar.	'Your father has already given up running for office.'
Seu pai já desistiu de se candidatar?	'Has your father already given up running for office?'

Ela já tem um freezer.   'She already has a freezer.'
Ela já tem um freezer?   'Does she already have a freezer?'

b. Listen again. Repeat aloud after each sentence.

c. Read each sentence aloud.

CD2 — track 36

d. Listen, then check the sentence you have heard: the declarative or the interrogative sentence.

DECLARATIVE

☐ *Tudo bem.*
   'That's OK.'

☐ *Choveu ontem.*
   'It rained yesterday.'

☐ *O doutor Nilo está em casa.*
   'Dr. Nilo is home.'

☐ *Depois do almoço voltamos ao trabalho.*
   'After lunch we'll go back to work.'

☐ *Esse novo funcionário é mesmo competente.*
   'This new employee is really competent.

INTERROGATIVE

☐ *Tudo bem?*
   'Is everything OK?

☐ *Choveu ontem?*
   'Did it rain yesterday?'

☐ *O doutor Nilo está em casa?*
   'Is Dr. Nilo home?'

☐ *Depois do almoço voltamos ao trabalho?*
   'Will we go back to work after lunch?'

☐ *Esse novo funcionário é mesmo competente?*
   'Is this new employee really 'competent?'

☞ **Check your answers with the Key.**

✎ A common mistake made by English speakers is to pronounce short verbal forms (*é, tem, vai*) as unstressed clitics, like English *is, has,* etc. In Portuguese, though, every verb must be fully stressed; otherwise, the sentence may become difficult, even impossible, to understand. In the following examples, the student should try to pronounce the verb forms (underlined) without rushing over them.

CD2 — track 37

e. Listen.

Essa garota <u>é</u> a melhor aluna da sala.	'This girl is the best student in the class.'
Ninguém <u>vai</u> gostar dessa sua decisão.	'No one will like this decision of yours.'
Meu carro <u>tem</u> o motor original.	'My car has the original engine.'
Aquela casa com a porta verde <u>é</u> do meu melhor amigo.	'That house with the green door belongs to my best friend.'
Minha enteada <u>tem</u> telefonado muito.	'My stepdaughter has been calling a lot.'

f. Listen again. Repeat aloud after each sentence.

g. Read each sentence aloud.

CD2 — track 38

h. A dialogue to memorize:

Um bom vendedor

[declaratives and yes-no questions]

Cena: na porta de uma casa
Personagens: vendedor e senhora

VENDEDOR: Bom dia. A senhora mora aqui?
SENHORA: Não senhor. Aqui é a casa da minha irmã.
V: Casa da sua irmã? E a sua irmã está?
S: Não; ela foi trabalhar e só volta de noite.
V: A senhora sabe se ela já tem aspirador de pó?
S: Já tem, sim senhor.
V: Ela tem freezer?
S: Tem sim.

Ela já tem vídeo-cassete?

V: Será que ela já tem vídeo-cassete?

S: Tem até dois.

V: Tem alguma coisa que a sua irmã ainda não tem?

S: Bom, ela não tem marido. Será que o senhor pode fazer alguma coisa?

V *[pensando]:* Pode ser. A senhora tem aí uma foto da sua irmã?

Lesson 29

Intonation: declarative sentences vs. topicalized sentences

🎵 Topicalized sentences (studied in *Modern Portuguese*, chapter 39) have a peculiar intonational contour. The topic, which comes at the head of the utterance, has a rising contour, followed by a sharp fall to the rest of the sentence, which shows normal declarative intonation (an exception is noted later in this lesson). In writing, the topic is often set off by a comma. In this lesson the topic is underlined.

CD2 — track 39

a. Listen.

Eu comprei esse bolo na padaria da esquina.	'I bought this cake at the corner bakery.'
Esse bolo, eu comprei na padaria da esquina.	'This cake I bought at the corner bakery.'
Eu faria qualquer coisa para você.	'I would do anything for you.'
Para você, eu faria qualquer coisa.	'For you I would do anything.'
Ele é inteligente, sem dúvida.	'He is intelligent, no doubt about that.'
Inteligente ele é, sem dúvida.	'Intelligent he is, no doubt about that.'
Eu costumo comprar o material em São Paulo.	'I usually buy the material in São Paulo.

> *Em São Paulo, eu costumo comprar   'In São Paulo I usually buy the
>   o material.*   material.'

b. Listen again. Repeat aloud after each sentence.

c. Read each sentence aloud.

Sometimes, especially in fast speech, the topic is not intonationally marked; it is run together with the rest of the sentence. The intonational contour in such cases is identical to that of normal declarative sentences.

CD2 — track 40

d. Listen.

> *Esse bolo eu comprei na padaria   'This cake I bought at the
>   da esquina.*   corner bakery.'
> *Para você eu faria qualquer coisa.*   'For you I would do anything.'
> *Inteligente ele é, sem dúvida.*   'Intelligent he is, no doubt about that.'
> *Em São Paulo eu costumo comprar   'In São Paulo I usually buy the
>   o material.*   material.'

i. Listen again. Repeat aloud after each sentence.

j. Read each sentence aloud.

CD2 — track 41

k. A dialogue to memorize:

Piquenique

[topicalized elements]

Cena: no parque
Personagens: Laurinha e Amanda

O que eu esqueci foi a manteiga

LAURINHA: Amanda, você trouxe o presunto?
AMANDA: Não. O presunto o Ricardo guardou na caixa de isopor. O queijo e os biscoitos eu trouxe, olha aqui eles.
L: E a sobremesa?
A: A sobremesa o Sérgio vai trazer. E o pão não deu tempo de comprar, porque nós saímos muito cedo.
L: O quê? Não tem pão? E como é que nós vamos fazer os sanduíches?
A: Ah, Laurinha! Isso você fala com o Sérgio, que ia trazer o pão.
L: Então o pão não foi você que esqueceu não?
A: Não. O que eu esqueci foi a manteiga.

Lesson 30

Intonation: wh-questions

> Wh-questions (*Modern Portuguese,* 31.1.2) are of three kinds: those with preposing of the questioned phrase, those without preposing, and those with *é que.*

Wh-questions with Preposing

> Wh-questions with a preposed questioned phrase have very similar intonation contours in Portuguese and in English. The questioned phrase (usually marked with one of the **wh-words,** *who, which, where, when, why*) comes at the head of the utterance and is pronounced with a higher pitch than the rest of the sentence is; the final intonation is falling. In the examples below the wh-word or phrase is underlined.

CD2 — track 42

a. Listen.

<u>Onde</u> você escondeu o casaco?   '<u>Where</u> did you hide the coat?'
<u>Para quem</u> esse sujeito trabalha?   '<u>Who</u> does this guy work for?'

O que a diretora vai usar na festa?   '<u>What</u> is the director going to wear to the party?'
Qual sapato te machuca o pé?   '<u>Which shoe</u> hurts your foot?'

b. Listen again. Repeat aloud after each sentence.

c. Read each sentence aloud.

Wh-questions without Preposing

> ✍ In wh-questions without preposing, the questioned phrase remains in its normal place in the sentence, as if it were not questioned. It is pronounced with a higher pitch than the rest of the sentence is, and the final contour is falling.

> CD2 — track 43

d. Listen.

Você escondeu o casaco <u>onde</u>?   '<u>Where</u> did you hide the coat?'
Esse sujeito trabalha <u>para quem</u>?   '<u>Who</u> does this guy work for?'
A diretora vai usar <u>o que</u> na festa?   '<u>What</u> is the director going to wear to the party?'

e. Listen again. Repeat aloud after each sentence.

f. Read each sentence aloud.

Wh-questions with <u>é que</u>

> ✍ Wh-questions can also be formed with the element *é que* after a preposed questioned phrase. Intonation is rising up to *é*, falling afterward. Wh-questions without preposing and those with *é que* are typical of the spoken language.

CD2 — track 44

g. Listen.

Onde é que você escondeu o casaco?	'Where did you hide the coat?'
Para quem é que esse sujeito trabalha?	'Who does this guy work for?'
O que é que a diretora vai usar na festa?	'What is the director going to wear at the party?'

h. Listen again. Repeat aloud after each sentence.

i. Read each sentence aloud.

CD2 — track 45

j. A dialogue to memorize:

Negócios com o governo

[wh-questions]

Cena: numa repartição pública.
Personagens: secretário e diretor.

SECRETÁRIO: Doutor, o seu Hélio ligou outra vez.
DIRETOR: O que é que ele queria?
S: Ele perguntou pelo pagamento.
D: Que pagamento é esse?
S: É do material de construção que ele forneceu.
D: Quando foi que ele forneceu esse material?
S: Foi no ano passado, deixa eu ver, em setembro.
D: E que dia é hoje?
S: Hoje é cinco de junho.
D: Como é que o seu Hélio quer que a gente pague com essa pressa toda? E eu que arranjei esse negócio pra ele! Onde é que está a gratidão desse sujeito?

Manda ele ligar dentro de um mês

S: O que é que eu respondo pro seu Hélio, doutor?
D: Pode falar que estamos providenciando. Manda ele ligar dentro de um mês.

Lesson 31

Intonation: choice questions, echo-questions, and tag-questions

Choice Questions

A choice question is one that presents two or more options. In Portuguese, as in English, the intonation is rising on all options but the last, which has a falling intonation.

CD2 — track 46

a. Listen.

Vocês querem leite ou café?	'Would you like milk or coffee?'
Ela vai falar de política, de cozinha ou de música?	'Is she going to speak about politics, cooking, or music?'
Quem vai falar é a diretora ou o senador?	'Who is going to speak, the director or the senator?'

b. Listen again. Repeat aloud after each sentence.

c. Read each sentence aloud.

111

Echo-Questions

Echo-questions (*Modern Portuguese,* 31.1.3) are used to convey the idea that the listener has not heard or understood what the speaker said; or that the listener can hardly believe his or her ears. In the written language, echo-questions are identical to yes-no questions or to wh-questions without preposing, but in the spoken language the intonation contour is different. Echo-questions always include a sharply rising intonation, usually accompanied by an increase in intensity, sometimes noted by '**??**', or '**?!**' (here I will always use '**??**'). This contour coincides with the questioned phrase in wh-questions; in yes-no questions it may occur with any major constituent—whichever is the focus of the request or of the incredulity.

CD2 — track 47

d. Listen.

Esse bolo foi feito <u>com fubá</u>??	'This cake was made with <u>cornmeal</u>?'
<u>*Esse bolo*</u> *foi feito com fubá??*	'<u>This cake</u> was made with cornmeal?'
Você escondeu o casaco <u>onde</u>??	'You hid the coat <u>where</u>?'
O cachorro <u>comeu</u> o chinelo??	'The dog <u>ate</u> the slipper?'

e. Listen again. Repeat aloud after each sentence.

f. Read each sentence aloud.

Tag-Questions

Tag-questions (*Modern Portuguese,* 31.1.4) have a rising final intonation, both when built with a repetition of the verb in the preceding sentence and when built with the all-purpose elements *não é?* and *né?* They do not occur with a falling intonation, as is sometimes the case in English.

CD2 — track 48

g. Listen.

Ela comprou um carro novo, não comprou?	'She bought a new car, didn't she?'
Ela não limpou nada, limpou?	'She didn't clean anything, did she?'
Ela comprou um carro novo, não é?	'She bought a new car, didn't she?'
Ela não entendeu nada, né?	'She didn't understand a thing, did she?'

h. Listen again. Repeat aloud after each sentence.

i. Read each sentence aloud.

CD2 — track 49

j) Listen, then check the sentence you have heard: the declarative or the interrogative one.

DECLARATIVE	INTERROGATIVE (CHOICE)
☐ *Vou comer peixe ou carne.* 'I'm going to eat fish or meat.'	☐ *Vou comer peixe ou carne?* 'Am I going to eat fish or meat?'
☐ *Quem chegou foi Zé ou Pedro.* 'Either Zé or Pedro arrived.'	☐ *Quem chegou foi Zé ou Pedro?* 'Who arrived, Zé or Pedro?'
☐ *Você telefona amanhã ou depois.* 'You'll call tomorrow or the day after.'	☐ *Você telefona amanhã ou depois?* 'Will you call tomorrow or the day after?'

DECLARATIVE	INTERROGATIVE (ECHO-QUESTION)
☐ *Seu pai escreveu esse livro.* 'Your father wrote this book.'	☐ *Seu pai escreveu <u>esse livro</u>??* 'Your father wrote <u>this book</u>?'
☐ *Seu pai escreveu esse livro.* 'Your father wrote this book.'	☐ *<u>Seu pai</u> escreveu esse livro??* '<u>Your father</u> wrote this book?'

□ *Vamos comer peixe amanhã.*
'We'll eat fish tomorrow.'

□ *Vamos comer peixe <u>amanhã</u>??*
'We'll eat fish <u>tomorrow</u>?'

□ *Vamos comer peixe amanhã.*
'We'll eat fish tomorrow.'

□ *Vamos comer <u>peixe</u> amanhã??*
'We'll eat <u>fish</u> tomorrow?'

☛ **Check your answers with the Key.**

CD2 — track 50

k. Listen, then check the sentence you have heard: the plain question or the echo-question.

PLAIN QUESTION

□ *Você fez o quê?*
'What did you do?'

□ *A Sílvia está morando onde?*
'Where is Sílvia living?'

□ *O elefante fugiu do zoológico?*
'Did the elephant escape from the zoo?'

□ *Amanhã vai chover?*
'Is it going to rain tomorrow?'

ECHO-QUESTION

□ *Você fez <u>o quê</u>??*
'You did <u>what</u>?'

□ *A Sílvia está morando <u>onde</u>??*
'Sílvia is living <u>where</u>?'

□ *O elefante fugiu <u>do zoológico</u>??*
'The elephant escaped <u>from the zoo</u>?'

□ *Amanhã vai <u>chover</u>??*
'It is going to <u>rain</u> tomorrow?'

☛ **Check your answers with the Key.**

CD2 — track 51

l. A dialogue to memorize:

Invasão

[wh-questions and echo-questions]

Cena: numa nave espacial
Personagens: marciano 1 e marciano 2

MARCIANO 1: Tudo pronto pro desembarque, chefe.

MARCIANO 2: A equipe de matança e destruição está a postos?

M 1: Não, chefe. Eles estão todos na enfermaria.

M 2: Eles estão aonde??

M 1: Na enfermaria, chefe. Foi por causa da visita de reconhecimento que fizeram ontem.

M 2: Como é que vamos desembarcar sem a equipe de matança e destruição?

M 1: É que eles pediram para passar o dia na praia. Aí comeram uns acarajés . . .

M 2: Comeram o quê??

M 1: Acarajés. É uma especialidade local; feitos com camarão, pimenta e azeite de dendê.

M 2: Azeite de quê??

Aí comeram uns acarajés . . .

M 1: De dendê, chefe. É muito gostoso. Mas às vezes dá dor de barriga.

M 2: E como é que nós vamos desembarcar? Só nós dois?? Esses nativos vão nos li-
quidar num instante! Vamos de volta pra Marte, já!

M 1: Tenho uma idéia melhor, chefe.

M 2: Uma idéia melhor?? Nós estamos em perigo, lembra disso!

M 1: Que nada, chefe. A gente volta pra Marte amanhã. Hoje a gente podia passar
o dia na praia, comer uns acarajés . . .

Lesson 32

Dialogues to memorize

✒ To sum up the lessons, here are some more dialogues to memorize. These dialogues have not been controlled as to difficulty and should be studied after completing the rest of the lessons.

CD2 — track 52

a. A dialogue to memorize:

Dor no olho

Cena: num consultório médico
Personagens: paciente e médico

PACIENTE: Doutor, essa dor no olho está me incomodando já faz muito tempo.
MÉDICO *[anotando]:* É uma dor constante?
P: Não, doutor, só dói quando eu tomo café.
M *[estranhando]:* Só quando toma café? Nunca ouvi falar disso.
P: É, doutor, mas é assim mesmo. Quando eu tomo café me dá uma dor forte, fininha, em um olho.
M: Isso só vendo. Olha aqui, você vai tomar um cafezinho.
[M pega a garrafa térmica na mesa e serve uma xícara de café]

M: Aqui, toma esse café.

P: Já está adoçado?

M: Não. Pega aqui o açúcar.

[M entrega o açucareiro para P. P põe açúcar, mexe e toma o café]

P: Uuuui! Olha só, doutor, me deu a dor no olho outra vez!

M: Tudo bem, tudo bem. Já sei o que é.

P: É grave, doutor?

M: Não muito. É só pingar um pouco desse colírio no olho. E lembrar de tirar a colherinha da xícara quando tomar café.

Me deu a dor no olho outra vez!

CD2 — track 53

b. A dialogue to memorize:

O paradeiro da chave

Cena: em frente de uma casa, de madrugada
Personagens: esposa e marido [um pouco bêbados]

Marido: Que horas são?

Esposa: Tou sem relógio. Mas é capaz de ser umas três da manhã.

M: Cadê a chave da casa?

E: A chave tá com você.

M *[mexendo nos bolsos]:* Não tá não. Deve tar na sua bolsa.

E: Que bolsa? Eu saí sem bolsa. E esse vestido não tem nenhum bolso. Tem que tar com você.

M *[um pouco irritado]:* Se a gente não achar a chave vai ter que dormir na rua. Já olhei, não tá em nenhum bolso. Será que eu deixei cair?

[Procuram no chão]

E: Nada por aqui. Ah, já sei: você deixou no carro. Você sempre faz isso.

M: É mesmo. Agora eu lembro. Que bom ter uma mulherzinha de boa memória!

[M dá um beijinho em E e sai para ir pegar a chave no carro]

Cadê a chave do carro?

E *[se encostando na porta]:* Ainda bem que lembrei onde tá a chave. Não agüento mais de sono.
[M volta]
M: Cadê a chave do carro?

CD2 — track 54

c. A dialogue to memorize:

Fim de semana

Cena: na sala
Personagens: Elvira e Moacir [marido e mulher]

Você acha que eu sou pasto de pernilongo?

ELVIRA: Moacir, sexta-feira é feriado. Que tal fazer uma viagem?

MOACIR: Grande idéia, Virinha! Direto pra praia!

E: O quê? Você lembra o que aconteceu da última vez? Queimadura de segundo grau!

M: Ah, mas dessa vez eu vou tomar cuidado. Levo protetor solar.

E: Olha, tem um hotel-fazenda perto de Atibaia . . .

M: Hotel-fazenda? Você acha que eu sou pasto de pernilongo?

E: O que, então? Praia? Nesses dias a estrada vai ficar que é uma fila só. A gente vai levar umas seis horas pra chegar em Guarujá. E o ar condicionado do carro não tá funcionando.

M: Tá bem, tá bem. Você sempre vence. Quanto tá a diária do hotel-fazenda?

E: Da última vez era cento e vinte reais, diária completa.

M: E o hotel de Guarujá?

E: Ah, esse deve estar mais de cento e oitenta.

[M pensa um pouco]

M: Ô Virinha, passa na locadora e aluga uns quatro filmes bem bons, tá?

Key

to the Exercises

The Key gives answers to the exercises of the type "Check the word/sentence you have heard."

Lesson 9, g: *Sá, pó, bola, gasta, corta, Mota*
Lesson 12, g: *fé, cê, mel, céu, sede* 'thirst'
Lesson 12, h: *lê, sei, dê, rolei*
Lesson 13, g: *dó, sou, avô, corte* '(royal) court,' *solto* 'free'
Lesson 13, h: *show, popa, coxa, voltei*
Lesson 15, g: *fala, vela, rolha, fila, molha, pulha*
Lesson 15, h: *aliado, afilhado, olhava, raleava*
Lesson 16, g: *lá, sã, van, manca, abas, manta, grade, caça, machucando, catando*
Lesson 17, g: *Leda, violeta, encho, cedo, fendeu*
Lesson 17, h: *som, dou, boba, concha, otário*
Lesson 18, g: *vim, mi, ri, vida, finca, lipo*
Lesson 18, h: *o, um gato, o peixe, tuba, mundo, fuga*
Lesson 19, g: *cães, manha, pais, mães, baia*
Lesson 19, h: *sei, nem, a lei, lenha, ceia, tenha*
Lesson 20, g: *pão, cal, mal, senão, capitão*
Lesson 23, g: *médica, tônico, vomito, contínuo, magoa, Flórida, desânimo*
Lesson 24, j: *tato, abri, teú, pia, cantam, porém*
Lesson 28, d: *Tudo bem? — Choveu ontem. — O doutor Nilo está em casa. — Depois do almoço voltamos ao trabalho. — Esse novo funcionário é mesmo competente?*

Lesson 31, j: *Vou comer peixe ou carne? — Quem chegou foi Zé ou Pedro. — Você telefona amanhã ou depois? — Seu pai escreveu <u>esse livro</u>?? — Seu pai escreveu esse livro. — Vamos comer peixe <u>amanhã</u>?? — Vamos comer <u>peixe</u> amanhã??*

Lesson 31, k: *Você fez o quê? — A Sílvia está morando <u>onde</u>?? — O elefante fugiu <u>do zoológico</u>?? — Amanhã vai chover?*

Translations

of the Dialogues

To give the translations some of the naturalness of the spoken language, I have made them not quite literal.

Lesson 15

On the beach

Scene: on the beach
Characters: Guto (boy) and Tê (girl)

Tê: Man, Guto, I can't believe this heat!
GUTO: Hold on. I'll get the beach umbrella.
T: But where is the umbrella?
G: It's in the car.
T: It's in the car? Where's the car?
G: It's right over there. . . . Hey! Where's the car? Either it was towed, or it was stolen!
T: What now? Walk home?
G: Walk. Nothing to it, babe. Only a three- or four-hour walk. It'll be nice.
T: Yeah, I wanted to get a tan, but this is ridiculous.

Lesson 18

The new job

Scene: at the office
Characters: Tita and the boss

Boss: Tita, this is your desk.
Tita: I already noticed. I got here early this morning.
B: Early this morning? In that case, you can get started.
T: Sure, I can start. That way the job will be done faster.
B: Hey, Tita, will you need paint?
T: Only later. I'll read the text first.
B: What then?
T: After I read it, then I'll work up some drawings. They'll be beautiful, you can be sure of that.
B: I sure hope so. The old designer was useless; she was even kind of stupid.
T: She was stupid, but I have been at this for several years.

Lesson 20

Handyman

Scene: at home
Characters: Carla and João

João *[arriving home, irritated]:* Now it's the garage door! It's broken! I had to leave the car on the street in this blazing sun.
Carla: João, João, honey! Why are you so irritated?
J: The garage door! The remote control doesn't work, and I can't open it manually.
C: Should I call an electrician?
J: No! I spent too much last week getting the kitchen floor fixed. And that cost a bundle. The garage door will have to wait until next month.
C: Maybe I can get the door open.
J: You? If I'm the engineer and can't get it open, what makes you think you can?
C: Come on, João. You're a civil engineer; you don't know anything about remote-controlled garage doors. Look, give me the remote.

[C opens the remote]
C: I've fixed the remote, Mr. Engineer.
J: Have you changed professions?
C: No. I only changed the battery.

Lesson 22

The big game

Scene: in the locker room
Characters: Fred and his coach (Sidney)

SIDNEY: Look, Fred, one more like this and I'll take you off the team! Losing in the last set!
FRED: But, Sidney, it could have happened to anyone.
S: What happened?
F: I tried that play I invented in the States. It worked several times before and has become a standard play.
S: But this time the ball hit the floor, didn't it?
F: I was tired out in the last set. I was all stressed out. I had a talk with the lawyer this morning.
S: You should make up your mind: either divorce or table tennis.
F: I'm calmer now. By the next match I'll be back in stride. I'll kill 'em.
S: You'd better, Fred. If not, you won't have your chance to go to the Olympics.
F: My business with Margaret will be settled this week. Then the climate will get better.
S: But remember: the ball is on the table, not on the floor. This is table tennis, not golf.
F: Leave it to me, Sidney. The most interested party in this deal is me: it's my reputation that's at stake.

Lesson 25

Pasta with eggs

Scene: in the kitchen
Characters: Mom and Lucinha

LUCINHA: Mom, how do you make pasta with eggs?

MOM: Pasta with eggs? Well, the same as pasta without eggs, except with eggs.

L: Can we put as much salt as we please in the mix?

M: Of course not, Lucinha. Just half a teaspoon.

L: And the eggs? Do you just break them, throw them in the mix, and start blending?

M: You blend them in until it's yellow.

L [*beating*]: Gee, Mom, the batter is a horrible color.

M: If you beat it slowly, the dough will be all lumpy. You have to beat hard.

L: Come over here, Mom. Is it all right now?

M: Let me beat it, Lucinha. What incompetence!

L: Some day I'll learn, Mom.

Lesson 27

The accident

Scene: on the street

Characters: policeman and witness

POLICEMAN: Ma'am, did you see the accident?

WITNESS: Yes, I did, Officer. I was going into the cathedral when I heard a loud braking noise. At that moment the car ran over the young man.

P: Was the vehicle speeding?

W: No, Officer. I think the tourist was not paying attention to the traffic and was caught by surprise. I ran to the telephone, called the hospital, and waited until the ambulance arrived.

P: Tourist? Do you think he is a tourist?

W: Yes. I first went to the drugstore to buy some aspirin, and he was there. Nobody understood what he wanted until he pointed to a chocolate bar and said, "How much is it?"

P: Could he be an American?

W: He looked more like a Japanese to me. I hope he wasn't hurt too badly.

P: I think he's only got a broken arm. It could have been worse.

W: Look over there on the ground!

P: What is it?

W: It's the chocolate bar! He didn't have time to eat it.

Lesson 28

A good salesman

Scene: at the door of a house
Characters: salesman and woman

SALESMAN: Good morning. Do you live here, ma'am?
WOMAN: No. This is my sister's house.
S: Your sister's house? And is your sister in?
W: No, she's at work and will not be back until evening.
S: Do you know if she already has a vacuum cleaner?
W: Yes, she does.
S: Does she have a freezer?
W: Yes, she does.
S: Does she have a VCR?
W: She even has two.
S: Is there anything that your sister doesn't have?
W: Well, she doesn't have a husband. Is there anything you can do about that?
S *[thinking]:* Maybe. Do you have a picture of your sister?

Lesson 29

Picnic

Scene: in the park
Characters: Laurinha and Amanda

LAURINHA: Amanda, did you bring the ham?
AMANDA: No. Ricardo put the ham in the cooler. I brought the cheese and crackers. See?
L: What about dessert?
A: Sérgio is going to bring the dessert. And I didn't have enough time to buy the bread because we left too early.
L: What? No bread? And what are we supposed to make sandwiches with?
A: Hey, Laurinha, you take the subject up with Sérgio, who was supposed to be in charge of the bread.

L: So it wasn't you who forgot the bread?
A: No. I forgot the butter.

Lesson 30

Business with the government

Scene: in a government office
Characters: secretary and director

SECRETARY: Sir, Hélio called again.
DIRECTOR: What did he want?
S: He asked about the payment.
D: What payment is that?
S: It's for the construction material that he supplied.
D: When did he supply this material?
S: It was last year, let me see, in September.
D: What day is today?
S: Today is June 5.
D: How is it that Hélio wants us to pay him so quickly? And I was the one who got him this business! Where's this guy's gratitude?
S: What do you want me to tell him, sir?
D: You can say that we are taking care of it. Tell him to call back in a month.

Lesson 31

Invasion

Scene: in a spaceship
Characters: Martian 1 and Martian 2

MARTIAN 1: Everything is ready for disembarkation, Chief.
MARTIAN 2: Is the kill and destroy team in place?
M 1: No, Chief. They're all in the infirmary.
M 2: They're where?
M 1: In the infirmary, Chief. It was because of that reconnaissance mission they went on yesterday.

M 2: How are we going to land without a kill and destroy team?

M 1: It's because they asked to go to the beach yesterday. And they ate some acarajé . . .

M 2: They ate what?

M 1: Acarajé. It's a local delicacy made from shrimp, pepper, and dendê oil.

M 2: What kind of oil?

M 2: Dendê, Chief. It's really good. But sometimes you get a bellyache from it.

M 2: And how are we going to disembark? Just the two of us? These natives are going to kill us in a minute. Let's return to Mars at once!

M 1: I have a better idea, Chief.

M 2: A better idea? We are in danger here, remember that!

M 1: No way, Chief. We can go back to Mars tomorrow. Today we can spend the day at the beach, eat some acarajé . . .

Lesson 32a

A pain in the eye

Scene: at the doctor's office
Characters: patient and doctor

PATIENT: Doctor, this pain in my eye has been bothering me for some time now.

DOCTOR *[taking notes]:* Is the pain constant?

P: No, Doctor, only when I drink coffee.

D *[surprised]:* Only when you drink coffee? I've never heard of that before.

P: Well, Doctor, that's what happens. When I drink coffee, I get a strong, sharp pain in one eye.

D: I'll have to see this. I'd like you to drink some coffee.

[D gets a coffee pot off the table and serves a cup of coffee]

D: Here, drink this coffee.

P: Does it already have sugar?

D: No. Take some sugar.

[D hands the sugar bowl to P. P adds sugar, then stirs and drinks the coffee]

P: Ouch! See, Doctor, it gave me another pain in my eye!

D: All right, all right. I already know what the matter is.

P: Is it serious, Doctor?

D: Not very. Just use these eyedrops. And remember to take the spoon out of the cup when you drink your coffee.

Lesson 32b

The whereabouts of the keys

Scene: in front of a house after midnight
Characters: husband and wife (both slightly drunk)

HUSBAND: What time is it?
WIFE: I don't have my watch on. But it's likely to be about three o'clock in the morning.
H: Where are the keys to the house?
W: You have the keys.
H *[searching in his pockets]:* They're not here. They must be in your purse.
W: What purse? I didn't bring one. And this dress has no pockets. You must have them.
H *[a little irritated]:* If we don't find the keys, we'll have to sleep on the street. I've already looked, and they're not in any pocket. Do you suppose I dropped them somewhere?
W: Nothing around here. Ah, I know: you left them in the car. You always do that.
H: Right. Now I remember. It's so nice to have a wife with a good memory!
[H kisses W and goes to get the keys in the car]
W *[leaning against the door]:* I'm glad I remembered where the keys are. I can't keep awake any more.
[H returns]
H: Where are the car keys?

Lesson 32c

Weekend

Scene: in the living room
Characters: Elvira and Moacir (wife and husband)

ELVIRA: Moacir, Friday is a holiday. How about taking a trip?
MOACIR: Great idea, Virinha! We'll go straight to the beach.
E: What? Do you remember what happened last time? Second-degree sunburn!
M: Yeah, but this time I'll be careful. I'll take sunscreen with me.

E: Look, there's a country inn close to Atibaia.

M: Country inn? Do you think I am a landing field for mosquitoes?

E: What else, then? The beach? This time of year the road will be packed. It will take us about six hours to get to Guarujá. And the car's air conditioning isn't working.

M: OK, OK. You always win. How much is the daily rate at this country inn?

E: Last time it was a hundred and twenty reals, room and board.

M: And in Guarujá?

E: Well, it must be above one eighty.

[M thinks a little while]

M: Hey, Virinha, why don't you drop by the video store and pick up four good movies?